Early reactions to *T*
Doctrine at 200 and What to Replace it With:

"David Swanson aptly deconstructs the imperial fiat which arrogates to the U.S. the unilateral authority to intervene in the affairs of sovereign states in the Western Hemisphere and to exclude any rival power from meddling in what is viewed as Washington's backyard. Far from giving the 200-year-old doctrine a decent burial, the U.S. has extended it globally."
—Roger D. Harris, Task Force on the Americas

"With his characteristic acerbic wit, Swanson demonstrates that the Monroe Doctrine carries malice and intentionally manipulative and lethal capabilities. As with many of his other writings, not only does Swanson offer scathing critiques of the Monroe Doctrine, he also offers solutions for the damage it has done that are readily handy and straightforward if we ever become courageous enough and willing to implement them."
—Tim Pluta, World BEYOND War

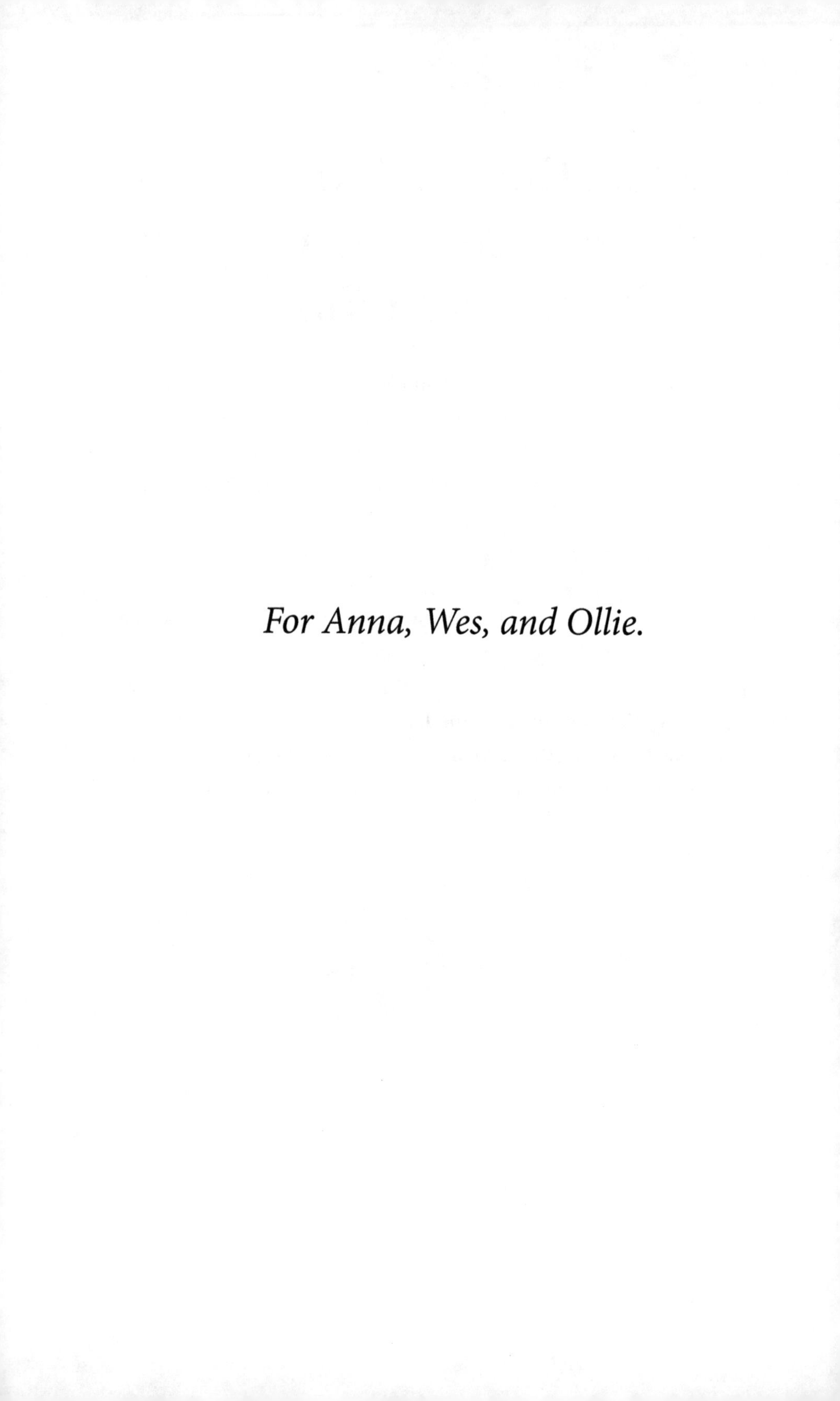

For Anna, Wes, and Ollie.

The Monroe Doctrine at 200 and What to Replace it With

By David Swanson

Charlottesville, Virginia
First edition—2023

Also by David Swanson

Snippers Saves the World (2021). ISBN 978-1734783704
Leaving World War II Behind (2021). ISBN 978-1734783759
20 Dictators Currently Supported by the U.S. (2020). ISBN 978-1734783797
Curing Exceptionalism (2018). ISBN 978-0998085937
War Is Never Just (2016). ISBN 978-0998085906
War Is A Lie (2010, 2016). ISBN 978-1682570005
Killing Is Not A Way of Life (2014). ISBN 978-0983083061
War No More: The Case For Abolition (2013). ISBN 978-0983083054
Tube World (2012). Illustrated by Shane Burke. ISBN 978-0983083047
The Military Industrial Complex at 50 (2011). Editor and contributor. ISBN 978-0983083078
When The World Outlawed War (2011). ISBN 978-0983083092
Daybreak: Undoing the Imperial Presidency and Forming a More Perfect Union (2009). ISBN 978-1583228883
The 35 Articles of Impeachment (2008). Introduction. ISBN 978-1932595420

Swanson, David, 1969 Dec. 1-
The Monroe Doctrine at 200 and What to Replace it With
Book and cover design by David Swanson
Cover image: altered from Wikimedia https://commons.wikimedia.org/wiki/File:World_map_longlat-simple.svg

Printed in the USA First Edition / January 2023
ISBN: 979-8-9869811-0-9

Contents

1. Why Does the Monroe Doctrine Matter?

Actions require justifications, but they require less justification the longer they've been understood as already justified. They can even lose their original justifications and continue to be engaged in, almost unquestioned but picking up novel justifications as needed.

The Monroe Doctrine was and is a justification for actions, some good, some indifferent, but the overwhelming bulk reprehensible. The Monroe Doctrine remains in place, both explicitly and dressed up in novel language. Additional doctrines have been built on its foundations. Here are the words of the Monroe Doctrine, as carefully selected from President James Monroe's State of the Union Address on December 2, 1823:[1]

> *"The occasion has been judged proper for asserting, as a principle in which the rights and interests of the United States are involved, that the American continents, by the free and independent condition which they have assumed and maintain, are henceforth not to be considered as subjects for future colonization by any European powers. . . .*
>
> *"We owe it, therefore, to candor and to the amicable relations existing between the United States and those powers to declare that we should consider any attempt on their part to extend their system to any portion of this hemisphere as dangerous to our peace and safety. With the existing colonies or dependencies of any European power, we have not interfered and shall not interfere. But with the Governments who have declared their independence and maintained it, and whose independence we have, on great consideration and on*

> *just principles, acknowledged, we could not view any interposition for the purpose of oppressing them, or controlling in any other manner their destiny, by any European power in any other light than as the manifestation of an unfriendly disposition toward the United States."*

These were the words later labeled the "Monroe Doctrine." They were lifted from a speech that said a great deal in favor of peaceful negotiations with European governments, while celebrating as beyond question the violent conquering and occupying of what the speech called the "uninhabited" lands of North America. Neither of those topics was new. What was new was the idea of opposing further colonization of the Americas by Europeans on the basis of a distinction between the bad governance of European nations and the good governance of those in the American continents. This speech, even while repeatedly using the phrase "the civilized world" to refer to Europe and those things created by Europe, also draws a distinction between the type of governments in the Americas and the less-desirable type in at least some European nations. Much of this, as well as a U.S. commitment to staying out of Europe -- balancing the U.S. demand that Europe stay out of the Americas -- is found in parts of the speech not strictly identified as the Monroe Doctrine. The two parts of the Monroe Doctrine are separated by a great deal of the speech. The second part of the Doctrine is preceded by these words:

> *"The citizens of the United States cherish sentiments the most friendly in favor of the liberty and happiness of their fellow men on that side of the Atlantic. In the wars of the European powers in matters relating to themselves we have never taken any part, nor does it comport with our policy so to do. It is only when our rights are invaded or seriously menaced that we resent injuries or make preparation for our defense. With the movements in this hemisphere we are of necessity more immediately connected, and by causes which must be obvious to all enlightened and impartial observers.*

The political system of the allied powers is essentially different in this respect from that of America. This difference proceeds from that which exists in their respective Governments; and to the defense of our own, which has been achieved by the loss of so much blood and treasure, and matured by the wisdom of their most enlightened citizens, and under which we have enjoyed unexampled felicity, this whole nation is devoted."

The Doctrine is followed by these words:

"Our policy in regard to Europe, which was adopted at an early stage of the wars which have so long agitated that quarter of the globe, nevertheless remains the same, which is, not to interfere in the internal concerns of any of its powers; to consider the government de facto as the legitimate government for us; to cultivate friendly relations with it, and to preserve those relations by a frank, firm, and manly policy, meeting in all instances the just claims of every power, submitting to injuries from none. But in regard to those continents circumstances are eminently and conspicuously different. It is impossible that the allied powers should extend their political system to any portion of either continent without endangering our peace and happiness; nor can anyone believe that our southern brethren, if left to themselves, would adopt it of their own accord. It is equally impossible, therefore, that we should behold such interposition in any form with indifference. If we look to the comparative strength and resources of Spain and those new Governments, and their distance from each other, it must be obvious that she can never subdue them. It is still the true policy of the United States to leave the parties to themselves, in the hope that other powers will pursue the same course."

So, we have in the surrounding text that added meaning to the Doctrine, and in the Doctrine itself, a formalization of the idea that "defense" of the

United States includes defense of things far from the United States that the U.S. government declares an important "interest" in. This practice continues explicitly, normally, and respectably to this day. The "2022 National Defense Strategy of the United States," to take one example of thousands, refers consistently to defending U.S. "interests" and "values," which are described as existing abroad and including allied nations, and as being distinct from the United States or the "homeland."[2] This was not brand new with the Monroe Doctrine. Had it been, President Monroe could not have stated in the same speech that, "the usual force has been maintained in the Mediterranean Sea, the Pacific Ocean, and along the Atlantic coast, and has afforded the necessary protection to our commerce in those seas." Monroe, who had bought the Louisiana Purchase from Napoleon for President Thomas Jefferson, had later expanded U.S. claims westward to the Pacific and in the first sentence of the Monroe Doctrine was opposing Russian colonization in a part of North America far removed from the western border of Missouri or Illinois. The practice of treating anything placed under the vague heading of "interests" as justifying war was strengthened by the Monroe Doctrine and later by the doctrines and practices built on its foundation.

We also have, in the language surrounding the Doctrine, the definition as a threat to U.S. "interests" of the possibility that "the allied powers should extend their political system to any portion of either [American] continent." The allied powers, the Holy Alliance, or the Grand Alliance, was an alliance of monarchist governments in Prussia, Austria, and Russia, which stood for the divine right of kings, and against democracy and secularism. Weapons shipments to Ukraine and sanctions against Russia in 2022, in the name of defending democracy from Russian autocracy, are part of a long and mostly unbroken tradition stretching back to the Monroe Doctrine. That Ukraine may not be much of a democracy, and that the U.S. government arms, trains, and funds the militaries of most of the most oppressive governments on Earth are consistent with past hypocrisies of both speech and action.[3] The slaveholding United States of Monroe's day was even less of a democracy than is today's United States. The Native American governments that go unmentioned in Monroe's remarks, but which could look forward to being destroyed by Western expansion[4] (some of which governments had been as much an inspiration for the creation of the U.S. government as had anything in Europe[5]), were often more democratic than the Latin American nations Monroe was claiming to defend but which the U.S. government would often do the opposite of defending.

Those weapons shipments to Ukraine, sanctions against Russia, and U.S. troops based throughout Europe are, at the same time, a violation of the tradition supported in Monroe's speech of staying out of European wars even if, as Monroe said, Spain "could never subdue" the anti-democratic forces of that day. This isolationist tradition, long influential and successful, and still not eliminated, was largely undone by U.S. entry into the first two world wars, since which time U.S. military bases, as well as the U.S. government's understanding of its "interests," have never left Europe. Yet in 2000, Patrick Buchanan ran for U.S. president on a platform of supporting the Monroe Doctrine's demand for isolationism and avoidance of foreign wars.

The Monroe Doctrine also advanced the idea, still very much alive today, that a U.S. president, rather than the U.S. Congress, can determine where and over what the United States will go to war -- and not just a particular immediate war, but any number of future wars. The Monroe Doctrine is, in fact, an early example of the all-purpose "authorization for the use of military force" pre-approving any number of wars, and of the phenomenon much beloved by U.S. media outlets today of "drawing a red line." As tensions grow between the United States and any other country, it has been common for years for the U.S. media to insist that the U.S. president "draw a red line" committing the United States to war, in violation not only of the treaties that ban warmaking[6], and not only of the idea expressed so well in the same speech that contains the Monroe Doctrine that the people should decide the course of the government, but also of the Constitutional bestowal of war powers on the Congress.[7] Examples of demands for and insistence on following through on "red lines" in U.S. media include the ideas that:

- President Barack Obama would launch a major war on Syria if Syria used chemical weapons[8],
- President Donald Trump would attack Iran if Iranian proxies attacked U.S. interests[9],
- President Biden would directly attack Russia with U.S. troops if Russia attacked a NATO member[10].

Another poorly maintained tradition begun with the Monroe Doctrine was that of supporting Latin American democracies. This was the popular tradition that sprinkled the U.S. landscape with monuments to Simón Bolívar, a man once treated in the United States as a revolutionary hero on the model of George Washington despite widespread prejudices toward foreigners and Catholics. That this tradition has been poorly maintained puts it mildly. There has been no greater opponent of Latin American democracy than the U.S. government, with aligned U.S. corporations and the conquistadors known as filibusterers. There is also no greater armer or supporter of oppressive governments around the world today than the U.S. government and U.S. weapons dealers.[11] A huge factor in producing this state of affairs has been the Monroe Doctrine. While the tradition of respectfully supporting and celebrating steps toward democracy in Latin America has never died out entirely in North America, it has often involved firmly opposing the actions of the U.S. government. Latin America, once colonized by Europe, was recolonized in a different sort of empire by the United States. The time has come to say enough is enough!

A couple of notes on language:

"Latin America" is the most convenient phrase I have for everything south of the current United States, but it did not exist during the lifetime of James Monroe. "South America" came into popular usage in the United States not long after 1823, prior to which "America" was often used to refer to one single continent from the top to bottom of the globe -- though we know who arbitrarily chose which the "top" is.

"Democracy" is also not a word that appears in Monroe's speech. Just as he outlines what Europeans must not do, while saying nothing of what the U.S. government must do or not do, he vaguely opposes "the political system of the allied powers" and calls it "essentially different" but does not name what it is different from. If forced to use a word for the more desirable system, he might have used "republic." He refers to various South American nations in the speech as "republics." Of course, neither the United States nor any other nation is run by popular vote, and "democracy" in U.S. speech today is, at best, shorthand for a government with some degree of public accountability, and, at worst, shorthand for the United States and whoever its allies may be, regardless of the conduct of their governments.

Writers have been declaring the Monroe Doctrine dead since at least the 1930s. The expansion of the Doctrine by President Theodore Roosevelt known as the Roosevelt Corollary has been declared dead by presidents and restored by other presidents. The Doctrine itself was given a eulogy by Secretary of State John Kerry, speaking to the Organization of American States (OAS) in 2013.[12] But Kerry had previously claimed to U.S. lawmakers that "the western hemisphere is our backyard." Even following Kerry's speech, Bolivia expelled the U.S. aid agency USAID, with President Evo Morales remarking that the United States "probably thinks that here it can still manipulate politically and economically. That is a thing of the past."[13] During Kerry's tenure as Secretary of State, the U.S. government supported coup attempts in Egypt, Burkina Faso, and Ukraine. Between Kerry's tenure and this writing, the U.S. government has supported coup attempts in Bolivia, Venezuela, Mali, Guinea, Chad, and Sudan -- and in Peru just as I was writing these words.[14]

A search for "Monroe Doctrine" in news articles on Google in December 2022, turns up:

- a December 2, 2022, celebration and defense of the Monroe Doctrine on Fox News[15], which links to . . . a July 14, 2021, Fox News video arguing for reviving the Monroe Doctrine in order to "bring freedom to the Cuban people" by overthrowing the government of Cuba without Russia or China being able to offer Cuba any aid[16],
- a November 29, 2022, Fox Business article citing the Monroe Doctrine as justification for opposing a government of Venezuela that the U.S. government has long sought to overthrow[17],
- a February 12, 2019, article in *The Economist* using the Monroe Doctrine to explain why the government of Venezuela would object to being overthrown[18],
- a March 4, 2019, article in *The Washington Post* reporting on the U.S. National Security Advisor explaining that the U.S. can overthrow the government of Venezuela for being dictatorial, even while the U.S. supports dictatorial governments around the world, because Venezuela falls under the Monroe Doctrine[19],
- a February 24, 2022, article in *India Today* defending Russian warmaking in Ukraine on the grounds that the U.S. would justify similar actions near its borders using its Monroe Doctrine[20],
- A September 26, 2022, article in the Chinese *Global Times* reporting on the Russian Foreign Minister denouncing the United States for imposing a global Monroe Doctrine[21],
- A December 5, 2022, article in the *Herald Ledger* reporting on Kentucky requiring that schools teach the Monroe Doctrine[22],

- A November 28, 2022, article from the Heritage Foundation warning that elected leaders in Latin America might try to roll back the Monroe Doctrine when it's needed to oppose China, as it once opposed so well the Soviet Union[23],
- a November 30, 2022, article from Responsible Statecraft suggesting that understanding the U.S. insistence on the Monroe Doctrine would help one understand the Russian insistence on Ukraine staying out of NATO[24],
- a December 2, 2022, article from the Bangladeshi *New Age* arguing that the U.S. is hypocritical for not allowing Russia any Monroe Doctrine[25].

In the build-up to the 2003 war on Iraq, on February 18, 2003, pro-war columnist Max Boot argued that a Bush Doctrine of "preemption" was merely a logical extension of the Monroe Doctrine.[26]

In 2019, President Donald Trump declared the Monroe Doctrine alive and well, asserting "It has been the formal policy of our country since President Monroe that we reject the interference of foreign nations in this hemisphere."[27] While Trump was president, two secretaries of state, one secretary of so-called defense, and one national security advisor spoke publicly in support of the Monroe Doctrine.[28] National Security Advisor John Bolton said that the United States could intervene in Venezuela, Cuba, and Nicaragua because they were in the Western Hemisphere: "In this administration, we are not afraid to use the phrase Monroe Doctrine."[29] Remarkably, CNN had asked Bolton about the hypocrisy of supporting dictators around the world and then seeking to overthrow a government because it was allegedly a dictatorship. Bolton used the Monroe Doctrine as his defense, "reinterpreting" the Monroe Doctrine to justify the longstanding U.S. policies of overthrows in the Western Hemisphere and active support for oppression elsewhere. The *Washington Post*, in reporting on this, included not a word in opposition to the policies being justified, but suggested that mentioning the Monroe Doctrine out loud might be "counterproductive to U.S. aims in Latin America."

To my knowledge, the President Joe Biden administration has thus far not supported the Monroe Doctrine in words, only in actions.

Voices in Africa have recently expressed fears that NATO references to Africa as "NATO's southern flank" are frighteningly similar to U.S. uses of the Monroe Doctrine to treat South America as the United States' southern flank.[30]

An even greater number of news articles is found in a Google search for "Doctrina Monroe" than for "Monroe Doctrine." The Spanish references are universally negative, opposing U.S. imposition of corporate trade agreements, U.S. attempts to exclude certain nations from a Summit of the Americas, and U.S. support for coup attempts, while supporting a possible decline in U.S. hegemony over Latin America, and celebrating, in contrast to the Monroe Doctrine, the "doctrina bolivariana."

The Portuguese phrase "Doutrina Monroe" is in frequent use as well, to judge by Google news articles. A representative headline is: "'Doutrina Monroe', Basta!"

The Monroe Doctrine is still explicitly kept alive both within the United States and around the world. But the case that the Monroe Doctrine is not dead extends far beyond explicit use of its name. In 2020, Bolivian President Evo Morales claimed that the United States had organized a coup attempt in Bolivia so that U.S. oligarch Elon Musk could obtain lithium. Musk promptly tweeted: "We will coup whoever we want! Deal with it." That's the Monroe Doctrine translated into contemporary language, like the New International Bible of U.S. policy, written by the gods of history but translated by Elon Musk for the modern reader. It's one example of millions.

The U.S. has troops and bases in several Latin American nations and ringing the globe. The U.S. government still pursues coups in Latin America, but also stands by while leftist governments are elected. However, it has been argued that the U.S. does not any longer need presidents in Latin American nations to achieve its "interests" when it has coopted and armed and trained elites, has corporate trade agreements like CAFTA (The Central American Free Trade Agreement) in place, has given U.S. corporations the legal power to create their own laws in their own territories within nations like Honduras, has massive debts owed to its institutions, provides desperately needed aid with its choice of strings attached, and has had troops in place with justifications like the drug trade for so long that they are sometimes accepted as simply inevitable.[31] All of this is the Monroe Doctrine, whether we stop saying those two words or not.

The history of the Monroe Doctrine is a story of ever changing meaning and action, including some jerky hesitant steps of conflicting interests and enormous incompetence within the U.S. government, and yet some general trends -- some of the steadiest streams being exceptionalism, expansionism, and bigotry. While the Doctrine was labeled and celebrated, expanded and reinterpreted, long after Monroe spoke it, the seeds of virtually everything done in its name were present from the start, and most of the worst practices are still engaged in as I write these words.

We're often taught that the Monroe Doctrine wasn't acted on until decades after its articulation, or that it wasn't acted on as a license for imperialism until it was altered or reinterpreted by later generations. This is not false, but it is overstated. One of the reasons that it is overstated is the same reason that we're sometimes taught that U.S. imperialism didn't begin until 1898, and the same reason that the war on Vietnam, and later the war on Afghanistan, were referred to as "the longest lasting U.S. war." The reason is that Native Americans are still not treated as being and having been real people, with real nations, with the wars against them being real wars. The portion of North America that ended up in the United States is treated as having been gained through non-imperial expansion, or even as not having involved expansion at all, even though the actual conquest was extremely deadly, and even though some of those behind this massive imperial expansion intended it to include all of Canada, Mexico, the Caribbean, and Central America. The conquest of much (but not all) of North America was the most dramatic implementation of the Monroe Doctrine, even if rarely thought of as being related to it at all. The first sentence of the Doctrine itself was opposing Russian colonialism in North America. The U.S. conquest of (much of) North America, while it was being done, was frequently justified as opposition to European colonialism.

As we reach the 200-year mark, I propose that we reconsider what the Monroe Doctrine is, where it came from, what it changed, and how it has been changed and used and abused through these two centuries. I think we may even want to reconsider the practice of establishing presidential doctrines at all. So I'll begin with the question "What is a Doctrine?"

2. *What Is a Doctrine?*

Most frequently a doctrine belongs to a religion; second most frequently it belongs to a government. Here is a dictionary definition of doctrine: "a particular principle, position, or policy taught or advocated, as of a religion or government: Catholic doctrines; the Monroe Doctrine." If the Monroe Doctrine were the Monroe Principle, or the Monroe Position, or the Monroe Policy, it would sound quite down to Earth, subject to change, and open to questioning. As a Doctrine, however, it takes on a more permanent, quasi-religious authority. It sounds like the sort of thing one can only violate by carefully contorting one's arguments so as to claim not to be violating it. In fact, some very different politicians have done just that for two centuries.

Of course, the Monroe Doctrine is not a treaty or a constitution. It's not a law of any sort. It's not even a resolution of Congress. It's certainly not anything that's been publicly voted on. Worse, a nearly identical resolution introduced by Speaker of the House Henry Clay in 1824 was voted down by Congress, mainly on the grounds that it would have given presidents unconstitutional war powers.[32] The Monroe Doctrine was, therefore, contrary to the will of Congress. It was just some excerpts from a speech, a speech specifically opposing European governments that promoted religion, tradition, and the divine right of kings, and advocating instead for democracy. But these words were enshrined by public commentators, with support from subsequent presidents and other officials, as a "doctrine," and that was treated -- including by two centuries of Congresses -- as more powerful than anything Congress or the public could have possibly created.

When I do a web search for "doctrine," the first presidential doctrine I find is the Truman Doctrine, but before that I find Bible Doctrine and Army Doctrine. One of those you're supposed to believe on faith and the other because you've been ordered to. Surely, the Truman Doctrine is different. Surely, if it seems mistaken or nonsensical then you're supposed to dissent from it, violate it, reform it, mock it, replace it, or all of the above. I mean, as long as a president is not a god and a citizen is not a slave.

When President James Polk first used the phrase "Monroe's Doctrine," 22 years after Monroe had spoken the words of the doctrine, Polk was contrasting the Monroe Doctrine with the "doctrine of the balance of power," meaning the European threat to make sure more than one nation controlled the Western Hemisphere. So, a doctrine could be rejected as well as accepted. But Polk was holding up the Monroe Doctrine as an established and unquestionable truth that even his partisan opponents would, he hoped, dare not oppose.

Historian Jay Sexton, in his book on the use of the Monroe Doctrine through the 19th century, describes U.S. politics prior to the Civil War. Both the Whigs and the Democrats, he writes, sought to limit British and European expansion. "Neither took much note of the views of the other inhabitants of the Americas: Polk attempted to erase Mexicans from the territories he coveted (the lands seized from Mexico, Polk informed Congress, were 'almost unoccupied'); Clayton and Bulwer barely consulted the governments of Central America, despite the fact that they negotiated a treaty pertaining to their territory."[33] Sexton is describing bipartisan agreement on at least two and perhaps three doctrines, only one of which he names, the Monroe Doctrine. The other two are the Doctrine of Discovery and the Doctrine (often but not always referred to as a doctrine) of Manifest Destiny.

The Doctrine of Discovery -- the idea that a European nation can claim any land not yet claimed by other European nations, regardless of what people already live there -- dates back to the fifteenth century and the Catholic church. It was put into U.S. law in 1823, the same year as

Monroe's fateful speech. It was put there by Monroe's lifelong friend, U.S. Supreme Court Chief Justice John Marshall. The United States considered itself, perhaps alone outside of Europe, as possessing the same discovery privileges as European nations. (Perhaps coincidentally, in December 2022 almost every nation on Earth signed an agreement to set aside 30% of the Earth's land and sea for wildlife by the year 2030. Exceptions: the United States and the Vatican.)[34]

The Doctrine of Manifest Destiny did not yet exist as a known label in 1823. When it was popularized in 1845, it was generally opposed by Whigs. Yet, there existed, before, during, and after the period in which the term "Manifest Destiny" was commonly used a widespread consensus in Washington D.C. on the behaviors it justified. The U.S. Civil War, in fact, originated in a dispute over the status of slavery in future states, a dispute that depended on near-universal consensus in favor of the addition of more states.

The Monroe Doctrine is part of the sub-genre of doctrines called presidential doctrines. It is not only the most famous of these, but also the oldest. It created the idea of the presidential doctrine, and its content is fundamental to various presidential doctrines that followed. But what are all the presidential doctrines, and how have they been created? Why is there no schedule for releasing new ones? Why do some presidents have them and others not? Why are there disputes over what a particular president's doctrine is and even over whether a president has a doctrine? Well, presidents don't create their own doctrines. Other people, generally people with access to be heard in major media outlets, pick out the most imperialist or belligerent thing a president has said (or perhaps it is the thing most similar to an aggressive reading of the Monroe Doctrine), and nominate that as a new doctrine. Commentators bicker over it a bit, arrive at a consensus, and one of the worst principles articulated during a four-to-eight-year period is sanctified. However, in the case of the Reagan

Doctrine, it seems to have been nominated by right-wing, war-loving columnist Charles Krauthammer prior to President Ronald Reagan having said it at all.[35]

According to Wikipedia there are 14 presidential doctrines.[36] They belong to presidents numbers 5, 26, 33, 34, 35, 36, 37, 39, 40, 42, 43, 44, 45, and the current president, number 46. Clearly doctrines have recently surged, whereas for much of U.S. history there was only one. George H.W. Bush was the last president with no doctrine, possibly because the media liked to call him a "wimp." Nowadays, a new president has hardly unpacked at the White House before being assigned a doctrine, or a few competing doctrines from journalists vying to identify a winning idea. The idea will likely have been drafted by a speechwriter and will need to be selected and then approved by corporate media outlets, but will be named for a president.

The list of 14 is fairly inclusive, and most books and articles on presidential doctrines select only some of those 14. Universally included as one of the doctrines, but not named a doctrine, is the Roosevelt Corollary, named for President Theodore Roosevelt and treated as a modification of the Monroe Doctrine -- although arguably all presidential doctrines are modifications of the Monroe Doctrine. Other sources add presidential doctrines beyond those 14, such as the Polk Doctrine. Some include with presidential doctrines additional doctrines named for secretaries of state, such as the Stimson, Weinberger, and Powell doctrines.[37] Others hyphenate to add to the list, as with the Hoover-Stimson doctrine.[38] I've identified 24 presidential or presidential cabinet doctrines that have been promoted by U.S. corporate media. I've interspersed them through the pages of Chapter 5 below, and will return to the question of doctrines in Chapter 9.

3. *Who Was Monroe?*

As we will see, much of the credit for drafting the Monroe Doctrine is given to President James Monroe's Secretary of State John Quincy Adams. But there is hardly any particular personal artistry to the phrasing. The question of what policy to articulate was debated by Adams, Monroe, and others, with the ultimate decision, as well as the selection of Adams to be secretary of state, falling to Monroe. He and his fellow "founding fathers" had created a single presidency precisely in order to be able to place responsibility on someone.

James Monroe was the fifth U.S. president, and the last founding father president, following in the path of Thomas Jefferson and James Madison, his friends and neighbors in what's now called Central Virginia, and of course following the only other person to run unopposed for a second term, fellow Virginian from the part of Virginia where Monroe grew up, George Washington. Monroe also generally falls in those others' shadows. Here in Charlottesville, Virginia, where I live, and where Monroe and Jefferson lived, a statue of Monroe, once found in the middle of the grounds of the University of Virginia, was long ago replaced by a statue of the Greek poet Homer. The biggest tourist attraction here is Jefferson's house, with Monroe's house receiving a tiny fraction of the attention. In the popular Broadway musical "Hamilton," James Monroe is not transformed into an African-American opponent of slavery and lover of freedom and show tunes because he isn't included at all.

But Monroe is a significant figure in the creation of the United States as we know it today, or at least he should be. Monroe was a great believer in wars and militaries, and probably the greatest advocate in the early decades of the United States for military spending and the establishment of a far-flung standing army -- something opposed by Monroe's mentors Jefferson and Madison. It would not be a stretch to name Monroe the founding father of the military industrial complex (to use the phrase Eisenhower had edited down from "military industrial congressional complex" or, as peace activists have begun denominating it following the variation -- one among many -- used by my friend Ray McGovern, the Military-Industrial-Congressional-Intelligence-Media-Academia-Think Tank complex, or MICIMATT).

Monroe was a soldier from age 17 to age 23, and thought like a soldier from then on. Those were years of revolution, 1776 to 1781, during which he showed courage in battle and became a war hero who carried a British musket ball in his chest. He also saw the British burn New York City in 1776, as he would later see them burn Washington in 1814. War was an accepted inevitability. War was what advanced James Monroe's career. His answer to the horrors of war, as it often is, was better preparations for more war. His feelings for the British were never better than mixed.

Monroe was Governor of Virginia during Gabriel's Rebellion of 1800, when the enslaved attempted to act on the rhetoric of Thomas Jefferson and violently free themselves. Monroe responded with martial law and executions, followed by giving a major boost to Virginia's military spending. Monroe believed that a military threat existed within the United States as long as people of African descent were present. In addition to boosting military spending, he tried to ship black people he didn't own to Africa. He tried to ship some of those involved in Gabriel's Rebellion to Sierra Leone, where a private British company ran a colony of former slaves including people who had escaped to fight on the British side in the American revolution, some of whom had subsequently tried to settle in Nova Scotia, including at least one former piece of property of George Washington, a man named Harry. Monroe's idea of shipping Virginian slaves to Sierra Leone did not work out, because he wanted them to remain slaves, at least for some period of time, and Sierra Leone did not permit slavery.

Monroe was a Virginia imperialist as well as a U.S. imperialist, a supporter and defender of Charlottesvillian and genocidist George Rogers Clark.[39] As a war veteran, Monroe was given 5,533 acres of Kentucky by the U.S. government, which did not own it. He supported this practice of giving other people's lands to veterans. Monroe found in the need to "remove" Native Americans ever westward, as in the need to suppress slave rebellions, an opportunity to counter accusations of hypocrisy with violence and preparations for more violence.

The story of U.S. conduct in New York State during Monroe's presidency (1817 to 1825) probably lacks no outrage ever committed in Central America under the banner of the Monroe Doctrine. Monroe himself in 1784 had been the first member of the Congress of the Confederation to go "west" when he took a tour of New York state and Pennsylvania to explore the edges of the empire. When Monroe was president, nations of people who had assisted the United States in its revolution were forced to give up their land by their "great father" President Monroe, in the interests of profitable corporations like the Ogden Land Company, facilitated by modern transportation improvements like the Erie Canal (built between 1817 and 1825). In Ohio, the U.S. bribed chiefs to sell lands. In Indiana, native nations were forced out, west of the Mississippi. The decision mentioned above of Chief Justice Marshall (Monroe's schoolmate and pal growing up in Virginia) to treat the Doctrine of Discovery as law meant that Monroe and his bloodthirsty subordinate Andrew Jackson could take land from people who could be said not to legally possess it.[40] Marshall later, in 1831, would rule against the Cherokee Nation, citing the use of phrases like "great father" to claim that Indigenous nations were related to the U.S. government as a "ward" is to "his guardian."[41]

In his 1824 State of the Union Address, one year after having spoken the yet-to-be-named Monroe Doctrine, Monroe falsely claimed that indigenous people could not be "civilized" (though various nations had adopted the language, learning, literacy, dress, agriculture, religion, and beliefs of the settlers), falsely claimed that native people living among the settlers were dying out (though they were multiplying), and concluded that removal to the west was needed for the victims' own good (even though settlers were flowing constantly west to repeat the process). And the key tool to accomplish that humanitarian act would be (this would be a steady theme) military spending.[42]

As Secretary of State for President Thomas Jefferson, Monroe purchased Louisiana from Napoleon (whose coronation both he and Simón Bolívar had attended), more than doubling the size of the United States by buying land claimed by France under the Doctrine of Discovery. But that had not been the complete mission, as the United States had also wanted Florida, from Spain or France or whomever it could be gotten from, as long as they were European. Later, as president, Monroe kind of sort of gave Andrew Jackson permission to attack Florida while kind of sort of avoiding responsibility for it, thereby staying on the right sides of both the Congress and the public while advancing the triple aims of imperial expansion against a European power, Native American removal, and removal of a sanctuary for people escaping from slavery. Jackson destroyed some Seminole settlements and captured the Spanish fort at Pensacola, but did not destroy the Seminole nation or convince it to hand over anyone who had escaped from slavery. The Spanish were done, however, and the United States annexed Florida in 1819.[43]

In fact, the United States and Spain in 1819 agreed to a treaty called the Adams-Onís Treaty or the Transcontinental Treaty, or the Florida Purchase Treaty, or the Florida Treaty. It gave Florida to the United States and drew a boundary between Spain and the United States that jogged north and west from the Gulf of Mexico out to the Pacific Coast of Oregon. On the Spanish side was a huge area of Mexico that the United States would seize 27 years later. On the U.S. side was a huge area of land not belonging to the United

States, including the current states of Idaho, Oregon, and Washington State, places also claimed by Britain, and to which, in the Monroe Doctrine four years later, Monroe would deny Russia could have any right.

Monroe and many of his contemporaries lived with fears not only of resistance from the enslaved or the dispossessed, and not only of challenges from European militaries, but also of breakaway states on the model of Aaron Burr's escapade, or of breakaway states aligning with European powers, or of civil war over the divisive question of abolishing slavery. Monroe's answer to that last point was compromise to delay the crisis. He signed the Missouri Compromise into law. Monroe's answer on every point was militarism.

As an adolescent, Monroe had seen his family participate in a boycott to overturn the Stamp Act. Nonviolent action was everywhere in those years, both disruptive and constructive campaigns long before Gandhi would name them. The colonists waged nonviolent resistance campaigns against the Stamp Acts of 1765, the Townsend Acts of 1767, and the Coercive Acts of 1774, resulting in de facto independence for large portions of the colonies. The colonists used boycotts, rallies, marches, theatrics, noncompliance, bans on imports and exports, parallel extra-legal governments, the lobbying of Parliament, the physical shutting down of courts and offices and ports, the destruction of tax stamps, endless educating and organizing, and the dumping of tea into a harbor — all to successfully achieve a large measure of independence, among other things, prior to the War for Independence. Home-spinning clothes to resist the British empire was practiced in the future United States long before Gandhi tried it.[44]

The colonists didn't talk about their activities in purely Gandhian terms. They didn't foreswear violence. They sometimes threatened it and occasionally used it. They also, disturbingly, talked of resisting "slavery" to England even while maintaining actual slavery in the "New World." And they spoke of their loyalty to the King even while denouncing his laws and his opposition to slavery.

Yet they largely rejected violence as counter-productive. They repealed the Stamp Act after effectively nullifying it. They repealed nearly all of the Townsend Acts. The committees they organized to enforce boycotts of British goods also enforced public safety and developed a new national unity. Prior to the battles of Lexington and Concord, the farmers of Western Massachusetts had nonviolently taken over all the courthouses and booted the British out.

And then the Bostonians turned decisively to violence.

While we imagine that the Iraq War has been the only war started with lies, we forget that the Boston Massacre was distorted beyond recognition, including in an engraving by Paul Revere that depicted the British as butchers. We erase the fact that Benjamin Franklin produced a fake issue of the *Boston Independent* in which the British boasted of scalp hunting. And we forget the elite nature of the opposition to Britain. We drop down the memory hole the reality of those early days for ordinary nameless people. Howard Zinn explained:

"Around 1776, certain important people in the English colonies made a discovery that would prove enormously useful for the next two hundred years. They found that by creating a nation, a symbol, a legal unity called the United States, they could take over land, profits, and political power from favorites of the British Empire. In the process, they could hold back a number of potential rebellions and create a consensus of popular support for the rule of a new, privileged leadership."

In fact, prior to the violent revolution, there had been 18 uprisings against colonial governments, six black rebellions, and 40 riots.[45] The political elites saw a possibility for redirecting anger toward England. The poor who would not profit from the war or reap its political rewards had to be compelled by force to fight in it. Many, including enslaved people, promised greater liberty by the British, deserted or switched sides.

Punishment for infractions in the Continental Army was 100 lashes. When George Washington, the richest man in America and practically James Monroe's neighbor, was unable to convince Congress to raise the legal limit to 500 lashes, he considered using hard labor as a punishment instead, but dropped that idea because the hard labor would have been indistinguishable from regular service in the Continental Army. Soldiers also deserted because they needed food, clothing, shelter, medicine, and money. They signed up for pay, were not paid, and endangered their families' wellbeing by remaining in the Army unpaid. About two-thirds of them were ambivalent to or against the cause for which they were fighting and suffering.[46] Popular rebellions, like Shays' Rebellion in Massachusetts, would follow the revolutionary victory.

Neither James Monroe, nor any of his fellow elites, seem to have learned the value of nonviolent action, or to have ever doubted the wisdom of turning to violence. In fact, they learned that celebrating war would benefit their careers for the rest of their lives. Some of the most powerful words in support of the War of Independence were "Give me liberty or give me death!" invented in 1805, 30 years after Patrick Henry was alleged to have said them.[47] But Patrick Henry, like James Monroe, could have given people liberty by freeing the people he enslaved, something King George III, the villain of the Declaration of Independence favored doing. (As Henry's actual speech was not recorded, and since the phrase "Give me liberty or give me death" was invented 30 years after 1775 and five years after Gabriel's Rebellion, the "Death or Liberty" flag used in that rebellion, which historians claim was inspired by Patrick Henry, may just possibly have, on the contrary, inspired the words placed in Patrick Henry's mouth.)

According to King George III, "The pretexts used by the Spaniards for enslaving the New World were extremely curious, the propagation of the Christian religion was the first reason, the next was the Americans differing from them in colour, manners, and customs, all of which are too absurd to take the trouble of refuting." Regarding enslaving Africans, King George III wrote, "the very reasons urged for it will be perhaps sufficient to make us hold such practice in execration." George never owned slaves, and approved the legislation that abolished the slave trade in England in 1807. But at least 41 of 56 signatories to the Declaration of Independence, and 12 U.S. presidents, including 10 of the first 12 to hold that office, owned human beings.[48]

In 1763, Britain defeated France. King George III quickly decreed that any British settlements west of the Allegheny-Appalachian mountains must be abandoned. Settlers continued to pour over the mountains, steal Native Americans' land, and form militias. Needing to pay for more soldiers to stop the settlers, Britain created the Stamp Act in 1765. Revolution started brewing.

King George III, according to one biographer, "was the epitome of a constitutional monarch, deeply conscientious about the limits of his power. He never vetoed a single Act of Parliament, nor did he have any hopes or plans to establish anything approaching tyranny over his American colonies, which were among the freest societies in the world at the time of the Revolution: Newspapers were uncensored, there were rarely troops in the streets and the subjects of the 13 colonies enjoyed greater rights and liberties under the law than any comparable European country of the day."[49]

A major lesson for the revolutionary generation was that the demonization of an enemy sells. This would be re-used for the War of 1812 and countless others. While Canada and many other countries might gain their independence without a bloody war, the United States would gain independence, war mythology, and westward expansion, while retaining slavery. Plus, there would be plenty of opportunities to try to take over Canada in the years to come.

Still, at the time of the drafting of the U.S. Constitution, one common view was to forbid a standing army, and to retain only state militias, white male militias used for the repression of slave revolts as well as for westwarding ethnic cleansing. The Second Amendment to the U.S. Constitution reads:

> *"A well regulated Militia, being necessary to the security of a free State, the right of the people to keep and bear Arms, shall not be infringed."*

George Mason's original draft reads:

> *"That the People have a Right to keep and to bear Arms; that a well regulated Militia, composed of the Body of the People, trained to arms, is the proper, natural, and safe Defence of a free State; that Standing Armies in Time of Peace are dangerous to Liberty, and therefore ought to be avoided as far as the Circumstances and Protection of the Community will admit; and that in all Cases, the military should be under strict Subordination to, and governed by the Civil Power."*

Mason's Virginia Declaration of Rights had put it this way 12 years earlier:

> *"That a well-regulated militia, composed of the body of the people, trained to arms, is the proper, natural, and safe defense of a free state; that standing armies, in time of peace, should be avoided as dangerous to liberty; and that in all cases the military should be under strict subordination to, and governed by, the civil power."*

The Second and Third Amendments to the U.S. Constitution originated, in part, as restrictions on a permanent military. But James Monroe backed a permanent military, and his position won out, to say the least. Nowadays, of course, even George Mason University has military contracts.[50]

Monroe did not seek military preparedness under the misguided, but popular today, idea that doing so reduces rather than increases wars. Monroe sought wars. During the 1790s, unlike his Republican mentors and allies, he advocated for a new war with Britain. He wanted to invade Canada, occupy Bermuda, and take over access to the Mississippi. With only slowly growing support for this approach from Federalists or Republicans, Monroe would push this sort of warmongering for decades.[51] In 1810 as a member of the Virginia House of Delegates, he played on his war hero status to successfully urge Virginia to demand that Congress invest more in militarism and seize West Florida.

Monroe was Secretary of State for President Madison when they got the War of 1812 going. Congressman Samuel Taggart (F., Mass.), in protest of a closed-door congressional debate, published a speech in the *Alexandria Gazette* on June 24, 1812, in which he remarked: "The conquest of Canada has been represented to be so easy as to be little more than a party of pleasure. We have, it has been said, nothing to do but to march an army into the country and display the standard of the United States, and the Canadians will immediately flock to it and place themselves under our protection. They have been represented as ripe for revolt, panting for emancipation from a tyrannical Government, and longing to enjoy the sweets of liberty under the fostering hand of the United States." Taggart went on to present reasons why such a result was by no means to be expected, and of course he was right. But a group of Congress Members as eager for war with Britain as Monroe was got what they wanted and originated the term "war hawks" in the process.[52]

Monroe was learning the skills of starting wars. He ran around proclaiming that war with Britain was regretfully inevitable, while privately hunting for some means of getting it started.[53] This story is reminiscent of hundreds of others, including that day on which President George W. Bush told British Prime Minister Tony Blair that painting an airplane with UN colors and flying it low to get it shot at might help start a war on Iraq; he then did a press conference about how they were trying to avoid war. As plotters of the war on Iraq found a dubious informant called Curveball to tell them what they wanted to hear, Monroe and Madison found John Henry and his associate Paul Émilie Soubiran who gave himself the fake title and name le Comte Édouard de Crillon. These characters duped Monroe out of $50,000 of public funds for false claims of evidence of a British and Federalist plot to arrange for New England to secede from the United States. Having seen the weakness of the evidence, Madison nevertheless went ahead and made the false claim of its strength to Congress. The fraud was discovered, and yet the war was quickly launched anyway -- an important lesson and model for two centuries of U.S. governments if ever there was one.[54]

When experts at the U.S. Department of Energy in 2002-2003 refused to say that aluminum tubes in Iraq were for nuclear facilities, because they knew they could not possibly be and were almost certainly for rockets, and when the State Department's people also refused to reach the "correct" conclusion, a couple of guys at the National Ground Intelligence Center near Monroe's hometown of Charlottesville were happy to oblige. Their names were George Norris and Robert Campus, and they received "performance awards" (cash) for the service. Secretary of State Colin Powell (a guy with a Doctrine) used Norris' and Campus' claims in his U.N. speech despite having been warned by his own staff that they weren't true. One has to imagine Monroe looking on with pride.

The War of 1812 failed to take any of Canada or to protect U.S. shipping, and got Washington D.C. burned, but still somehow it boosted militarism and nationalism, especially through celebration of Andrew Jackson's victory in New Orleans which happened after the war was supposed to have been ended, and through the creation of a national anthem that celebrated a flag surviving a battle in which mere people died, as well as celebrating the killing of people who escaped from slavery. Another important lesson was learned.

The father of the MICIMATT saw which side his bread was buttered on. He sought to create a spy agency. He proposed creating a military draft (successfully blocked by Congressman Daniel Webster and others who denounced it as unconstitutional). He eventually obtained for the Department of War 35% of all government spending. He helped spend the U.S. government into debt, reversed his and his party's position to support a national bank, and did much to create that beloved institution known as taxation. Congress passed a tax program in 1812 that included a direct tax on land, and excise taxes on retailers, stills, auction sales, sugar, bank notes, and carriages. And in 1815, Congress added a new direct tax and restored the controversial whiskey tax, plus taxes on all kinds of items, luxurious and otherwise. The idea of an income tax was raised but rejected until required for the Civil War.

Monroe didn't just want military spending, and he didn't just want wars; he also wanted to be in the wars himself. He continually asked President Madison to give him a field command in the War of 1812 and eventually got himself made Secretary of War, where he demanded huge increases to the size of the military and its budget.

Monroe won the presidency in 1816 with a total of 183 votes, and began work on a permanent standing army and unsuccessful efforts to create a draft. He spent much of his presidential efforts on building bases and ships -- sending ships as far away as the Pacific and the Mediterranean. In the Mediterranean, Stephen Decatur commanded U.S. ships against Algiers in perhaps the first U.S. use of "gunboat diplomacy."

Monroe's presidency and entire political career as soldier, Delegate to the Congress of the Confederation, U.S. Senator, U.S. Minister to France, Governor of Virginia, U.S. Minister to the United Kingdom, Governor of Virginia again, Secretary of State, Secretary of War, and President were tied up in the expansion of U.S. territory, population, and power. And it was all from a very privileged position.

Monroe's day lacked today's concentration of wealth, but he lived in a class for which a shortage of bread in Paris was a problem for others, merely an annoyance for him to observe and contemplate. A Monroe biographer wrote of a new Monroe house in Paris, "Money was tight but Monroe spent lavishly on internal repairs and returning the gardens to their former glory. Five more servants, including a cook, were added to assist Polly and Michael. James and Elizabeth furnished the rooms with beds, tables, Louis XVI chairs, sofas, mirrors, and a commode, all simply designed but well constructed. Most of it came from the former homes of aristocrats, seized shortly after they were imprisoned. Elizabeth found a pianoforte and elegant Limoge china, while Monroe filled the small library with books, including the works of Voltaire, Rousseau, and Plutarch, all handsomely bound. He was particularly proud of a *secrétaire:* a false-front, mahogany desk with a marble top." Now I ask you, how tight does it sound like money was?

Monroe was a lifetime enslaver of human beings, who inherited some of them as property at age 16, who purchased Sally Hemmings' sister[55], and who eventually owned 75 people, bought and sold them, and rented them out. He never freed them. At the end of his life he sold them to pay his debt. Thomas Jefferson did the same. George Washington didn't die broke, and put the freeing of his slaves, following his wife's death, into his will. Monroe's failure to free his slaves was not, contrary to popular apology, because the 18th century mind could not grasp the very idea of freeing people from slavery.[56]

Not only were there slave revolts happening within the United States and on nearby islands of the Caribbean, but people in the United States were freeing everyone they owned and urging others to do the same.[57] One of the largest enslavers in Virginia and a friend of Jefferson, Robert Carter III, freed over 500 people. Another Virginia plantation owner named Robert Pleasants freed his slaves and wrote to Jefferson about it. Revolutionary war hero Tadeusz Kościuszko attempted to leave Jefferson funds with which to free Jefferson's slaves -- the failure of which effort is complex, the point being merely that the idea was clearly not unthinkable. It was being discussed and acted on.

In fact, Monroe was so aware of the possibility of freeing people from slavery, that he devoted a great deal of energy to doing something about those who were freed, namely trying to get them all shipped off to Africa, where the capital of Liberia would end up being named Monrovia in his honor. Monroe was a supporter of the Society for the Colonization of Free People of Color of America, later called the American Colonization Society. In 1822, the year before the Monroe Doctrine was spoken, colonizers established the Colony of Liberia, to which some 2,638 African Americans would migrate. They had U.S. funding and the help of the U.S. Navy thanks to President Monroe. Sadly and disastrously, the colonizers seem to have given as little thought to the people already living in Liberia as the British colonizers had given to the people already living in America.

Most presidential historians are myth makers. They'll tell you that Monroe was a very personable and likable character, very restrained and diplomatic. Maybe he was. Yet he nearly dueled with Alexander Hamilton. The dispute was probably resolved by the man assigned to be Monroe's second in the duel, Aaron Burr, who would later kill Hamilton himself, and whose view on Monroe was less than positive:

"The man himself is one of the most improper and incompetent that could have been selected — naturally dull and stupid — extremely illiterate — indecisive to a degree that would be incredible to one who did not know him — pusillanimous and of course hypocritical — has no opinion on any subject and will be always under the government of the worst men — pretends, as I am told, to some knowledge of military matters, but never commanded a platoon nor was ever fit to command one — 'He served in the revolutionary War' — that is, he acted a short time as aide de camp to Lord Stirling who was regularly drunk from morning to morning — Monroe's whole duty was to fill his lordship's tankard and hear with indications of admiration his lordship's long stories about himself — Such is Monroe's military experience . . . As a lawyer, Monroe was far below mediocrity — He never rose to the honor of trying a cause of the value of an hundred pounds."[58]

That's quite a contrast with Jefferson's view of Monroe as "a man whose soul might be turned wrong side outwards without discovering a blemish to the world."

In my view, Monroe's public service is of more interest than his personal character. John Quincy Adams praised Monroe by listing all of his actions to build up the U.S. military, including "controlling by a firm though peaceful policy the hostile spirit of the European Alliance against Republican South America," and concluding that Monroe "was entitled to say, like Augustus Caesar of his imperial city, that he had found her built of brick and left her constructed of marble."[59]

This so-called service amounts almost entirely to an uninterrupted blemish openly discovered to the world, a highlight of which is the Monroe Doctrine.

4. How Was the Monroe Doctrine Created?

Original intent can be a pretty poor way, but not a completely irrelevant way, to interpret an existing law. That Second Amendment mentioned earlier cannot have originally intended anything whatsoever, one way or another, about machines that could slaughter whole crowds of people in a matter of seconds without reloading. But it did intend -- and was generally understood to mean -- something about deadly weapons. The Monroe Doctrine cannot have originally intended that anything be done with robot death planes or nuclear-armed submarines. But it did intend something about relations between governments that used deadly ships, cannons, and guns.

In addition, the Monroe Doctrine has never been a law, and the rules for interpreting it over time have allowed modifying it beyond what anyone might have been constrained to argue was necessary or inevitable. There has also not been complete agreement on what words to consider the doctrine -- purely the excerpted passages or the speech as a whole -- or which contradictory ideas to uphold.

Nonetheless, a place to start in understanding the ongoing saga of an ever-evolving "doctrine" is with its creation, its early interpretation, and its early implementation.

By 1823, the United States had made various degrees of claim to large sections through the middle of North America, had tried repeatedly to claim Canada, had been given a chunk of Canada by Britain (Michigan, Wisconsin, Illinois, Ohio, Indiana), had made the Louisiana Purchase, taken Florida, and laid claim to territory all the way out to Oregon and Washington.

By 1823, the United States had used its military in significant actions in quite a number of places, against quite a number of nations[60]:

1774-1883 Shawnee, Delaware
1776 Cherokee
1777-1781 Iroquois Confederacy (Haudenosaunee)
1780-1794 Chickamauga
1790-1795 Miami Confederacy
1792-1793 Muskogee (Creek)
1798-1801 Naval war with France
1801-1805 Tripoli
1806 Mexico
1806-1810 Spanish, French privateers, Gulf of Mexico
1810 Spanish West Florida
1810-1813 Shawnee Confederacy
1812 Spanish Florida, Amelia Island
1812-1815 Canada (Great Britain)
1812-1815 Dakota Sioux
1812-1815 Iroquois Confederacy (Haudenosaunee)
1813 Spanish West Florida
1813-1814 Marquesas Islands
1813-1814 Muskogee (Creek) Confederacy
1814 Spanish Florida
1814-1825 Pirates, Caribbean
1815 Algiers
1815 Tripoli
1816 Spanish Florida
1817-1818 Spanish Florida, Amelia Island
1817-1819 Seminole
1818 Oregon (Russia, Spain)
1820-ongoing African Slave Trade Patrol
1822-ongoing Cuba (Spain)

These are only the major actions. A complete list could probably never be formed. Monroe had for years urged and had begun creating a "coastal defense" program, and that included the Pacific coast. It almost included the coast of Antarctica, the first recorded human sighting of which was in 1820, in which year Secretary of State John Quincy Adams urged Monroe to send a U.S. frigate to Antarctica to guard U.S. interests in the hemisphere against the British. However, they couldn't do it because most of their ships were in the Mediterranean.[61] The U.S. had already, during the War of 1812, attempted to claim islands in the middle of the South Pacific; that's what the reference to the Marquesas Islands is in the list above.

The idea of a U.S. hemisphere was not new to Monroe. He had been governor of Virginia when Jefferson had written to him with a vision of U.S. farmers who would "cover the whole northern, if not southern continent, with a people speaking the same language, governed in similar forms, and by similar laws; nor can we contemplate with satisfaction either blot or mixture on that surface."[62]

In 1821, Secretary of State John Quincy Adams told British Minister to the United States Stratford Canning that the United States would not threaten British Canada, and that Britain should "leave the rest of the continent to us."[63] In the same year, Adams told the Russian Minister to withdraw claims from North America, and that the United States was adopting the principle that "the American continents are no longer subjects for any new European colonial establishments." In 1823, at the same time that Monroe was planning his speech, he and Adams were agreeing on the very similar language for notes from Adams to foreign governments.

In cabinet meetings leading up to Monroe's 1823 State of the Union, there was much discussion of adding Cuba and Texas to the United States. It was generally believed that these places would want to join. This was in line with cabinet members' common practice of discussing expansion, not as colonialism or imperialism, but as anti-colonial self-determination. By opposing European colonialism, and by believing that anyone free to choose would choose to become part of the United States, these men were able to understand imperialism as anti-imperialism.[64] So the fact that the Monroe Doctrine sought to forbid European actions in the Western Hemisphere but said nothing about forbidding U.S. actions in the Western Hemisphere is significant. Monroe was simultaneously warning Russia away from Oregon and claiming a U.S. right to take over Oregon. He was similarly warning European governments away from Latin America, while not warning the U.S. government away. He was both sanctioning U.S. interventions and outlining a justification for them (protection from Europeans), a far more dangerous act than simply announcing imperial intentions.

This was a time of revolution in Latin America, in the Caribbean, and in Europe. The U.S. public had grown up on celebration of the U.S. revolution and was, at least in part, easily inclined to support similar revolutions to the south. Those in power in Washington had mixed views, wanting good relations with the European powers against whom the revolutions were fought, and with those European powers who saw benefits from defeats of their rivals, but also wanting to support democratic progress, while -- however -- viewing Latin Americans as ignorant and impoverished Catholics and primitives, and mostly hoping to somehow claim the whole hemisphere as their own.

Latin America's abuse by Europe had begun when Spain had rid its nation of Muslims and Jews while discovering continents to plunder in the name of God. Europe had grown rich from Latin American silver and gold, and the labor of enslaved Native Americans and Africans. The Spanish had claimed that enslaved labor was for the good of the subhuman Indigenous peoples.

Wealth extracting, forest-burning, soil depleting monocultural plantations for sugar, cacao, coffee, etc., and then oil, enriched Europe while destroying enslaved workers, creating feudalism, and placing whole economies subject to the price of a product. This was centuries of murder by poverty, not just by military. A new and different but significant wave would crash when the United States had rid the continental United States of resisting Native American and European nations. For now, the United States was otherwise occupied. But it had one eye on the revolutions to its south. Soon, U.S. presidents and secretaries of state would claim that ignorant Catholic South Americans were not ready for self-governance and needed to be dominated for their own good.

Already, John Quincy Adams was using this language in the abstract. In his famous speech on the Fourth of July 1821, the Secretary of State had said:

> *"For the independence of North America, there were ample and sufficient causes in the laws of moral and physical nature. The tie of colonial subjection is compatible with the essential purposes of civil government, only when the condition of the subordinate state is from its weakness incompetent to its own protection. . . . "*

In other words, colonialism is benevolent when imposed on incompetent people.

> *"The tie of colonial subjection may suit the relations between a great naval power, and the settlers of a small and remote Island in the incipient stages of society: but was it possible for British intelligence to imagine, or British sense of justice to desire, that through the boundless ages of time, the swarming myriads of freemen, who were to civilize the wilderness and fill with human life the solitudes of this immense continent, should receive the mandates of their earthly destinies from a council chamber at St. James's, or bow forever in submission to the omnipotence of St. Stephen's Chapel? . . . "*

In other words, the settler-colonialism of the United States, rolling westward, need not even be justified as being imposed on incompetent people, because there is nothing there but "solitudes." This is curious, not only because it's false, but also because , earlier in the same speech, Adams described colonial relations with the people of those "solitudes":

> *"Thus was a social compact formed upon the elementary principles of civil society, in which conquest and servitude had no part. The slough of brutal force was entirely cast off; all was voluntary; all was unbiased consent; all was the agreement of soul with soul."*

This is so false as to be extremely offensive, but it hints at a history that was becoming less and less talked about. Why, after all, should relations with the Indigenous peoples of North America, no matter how inaccurately characterized, be any sort of argument against British rule of the colonies, unless the Indigenous people added something valuable? In fact, when Europeans first learned about Native Americans, they also learned directly from them, through debates and discussions, written works and exchanges, public and private seminars, both in the Americas and in Europe. The indigenous critique of European society included its lack of freedom, equality, or fraternity, its shocking willingness to leave people poor and suffering, and its obsession with wealth at the expense of time and leisure. This critique, David Graeber and David Wengrow argue, was the origin of a great strain of thought in the European "Enlightenment," to which a major response was the Rousseau-Hobbesian infantilization of the people who had just made a wise, coherent, and articulate critique, as well as the invention of false claims of the necessity to sacrifice freedom for safety, of the supposed decrease rather than increase in hours worked after shifting to a European way of life, etc.

Prior to the critique made by the residents of Turtle Island, according to Graeber and Wengrow, European intellectuals didn't bother to make excuses for inequality as an inevitable sign of progress, because the notion that there was anything wrong with inequality hadn't much occurred to them. Many of the societies that were in great part wiped out for the creation of the United States were mutually recognized by both themselves and Europeans as free in comparison with Europe and its colonies; the only dispute was whether freedom was a good thing or not. Today, the Native Americans have basically won the rhetorical debate, while the Europeans have won the lived reality. Everybody loves freedom; few have it. Although if you utter the phrase "defund the police" you may discover vibrant remnants of those Jesuits who admitted that Wendat people had much less conflict than existed in France despite having to obey no laws, yet denounced that success as a matter of principle.[65]

According to John Quincy Adams, still in the same speech, the United States had always perfectly respected every nation it had admitted the existence of:

> *"She has, in the lapse of nearly half a century, without a single exception, respected the independence of other nations, while asserting and maintaining her own. She has abstained from interference in the concerns of others, even when the conflict has been for principles to which she clings, as to the last vital drop that visits the heart. She has seen that probably for centuries to come, all the contests of that Aceldama, the European World, will be contests between inveterate power, and emerging right. Wherever the standard of freedom and independence has been or shall be unfurled, there will her heart, her benedictions and her prayers be. But she goes not abroad in search of monsters to destroy. She is the well-wisher to the freedom and independence of all. She is the champion and vindicator only of her own. She will recommend the general cause, by the countenance of her voice, and the benignant sympathy of her example. She well knows that by once enlisting under other banners than her own,*

> *were they even the banners of foreign independence, she would involve herself, beyond the power of extrication, in all the wars of interest and intrigue, of individual avarice, envy, and ambition, which assume the colors and usurp the standard of freedom. The fundamental maxims of her policy would insensibly change from liberty to force. The frontlet upon her brows would no longer beam with the ineffable splendor of freedom and independence; but in its stead would soon be substituted an imperial diadem, flashing in false and tarnished luster the murky radiance of dominion and power. She might become the dictatress of the world: she would be no longer the ruler of her own spirit."*[66]

In other words, the U.S. government supports wars for independence but will not join in them, because there would be no end to the things, and they would transform the United States itself into something undesirable. I think that Adams was properly implying what we would later know from numerous examples to be the case, namely that when the U.S. government sided with an independence movement its goal would inevitably slip from independence to dependence on the United States rather than on Spain or some other power.

The first successful revolution south of the United States was in Haiti in 1791-1804. This one the U.S. government was largely opposed to -- not to say horrified of -- because people of African descent had freed themselves and taken over, inspiring other slave revolts across the region. The U.S. approach to Haiti ever since has ranged from open hostility to malign paternalism. Numerous successful and unsuccessful black-led revolutions swept the Caribbean in the mid-1790s. And in 1808 the wars for independence from Spain, led by Simón Bolívar, had begun, by 1823 establishing independent nations in much of Latin America, while at the same time Mexico won its independence in 1823, and Brazil was in the process of winning its independence by 1824. A continent was being transformed. The United

States was, in part, an inspiration for this transformation, but had almost nothing directly to do with it, and was rather confused about what to do about it.

During Monroe's presidency, statues of Simón Bolívar were put up around the United States. (There is also a monument to George Washington in Venezuela, as in Peru, Mexico, Colombia, and Argentina.) Towns were named for Bolívar across the rapidly growing U.S. and countless baby boys were named Simon -- a name that became as popular as George or Benjamin. At Fourth of July celebrations, girls wore Bolívar hats to hear speeches about Bolívar. Lafayette, whose wife Monroe rescued from a Paris jail along with Thomas Paine, sent Bolívar a portrait of George Washington from Washington's house and received in reply perhaps one of the most eloquent and extravagant thank-you notes ever written. Even much later, from the 1960s to the 1990s, the U.S. Navy patrolled the Caribbean with a ship named the U.S.S. Simón Bolívar. But by then "Bolivarian" was understood in Latin America to mean resistance to anti-democratic U.S. interference. Something went wrong in the hemisphere of democracy and brotherhood.

From the start, there was a problem. Bolívar was for U.S.-like independent and elected governments, but was not actually from the United States. He read the same Europeans that U.S. revolutionaries read. He used violent revolution and denounced monarchy. He even agreed with various North Americans that South Americans were not ready for democracy. He chose independence and unity over democracy. But he intended Jeffersonian language without Jeffersonian hypocrisy. He freed both governments from foreign monarchs and people, including Indigenous people, from slavery (but not from mandatory military service). He denounced Spain for the horrors it had committed since the arrival of Columbus, not just for a few recent pieces of legislation. He dreamed of creating a single, large, but Southern nation, and failed, creating instead a series of smaller nations in the areas that are now Venezuela, Ecuador, Bolivia, Peru, Colombia, and Panama -- a total area several times larger than the original United States. He was assisted by Haiti, Ireland, and Great Britain, but not by the U.S. government. He was depicted as deeply flawed and strange but infinitely good and sympathetic in a fictional portrait by Gabriel Garcia Márquez, but not as having superhuman strength or unfailing honesty or as even having gone near a cherry tree with an ax.

Brian Concannon Jr., Director of the Institute for Justice & Democracy in Haiti, tells me that "Haiti helped Bolivar twice. But when he had the chance to reciprocate, he bowed to the U.S. and excluded Haiti from the First Congress of the American States in 1826, setting the stage for the use of the OAS and other institutions to repress progressive politics in the Americas."[67]

Bolivar was not the only one to make compromises. According to Monroe biographer Tim McGrath, it was all right for Speaker of the House Henry Clay and others to insist on support for Latin American revolutions, but Monroe, despite privately supporting the revolutions, could not say so publicly because he was president -- he had no choice but to insist on neutrality. Yet the House agreed with Monroe by a vote of 115 to 45.[68] Of course Monroe did not wish to antagonize Spain while he was trying to negotiate Florida away from it. But it was over a year after he'd fully acquired Florida (and a claim of land all the way to the Pacific) that Monroe finally recognized the new nations of Buenos Aires (now Argentina), Chile, Colombia, and Peru, as well as Mexico, and asked Congress to fund the creation of embassies.

Presumably the motivations for recognizing the newly independent nations included that they had succeeded, that there was no longer a question of joining in wars, and that the U.S. had some sympathy and respect for the new countries. But those new countries were also being recognized by and forming alliances with other nations, and the United

States did not wish to be left out. Monroe did not want the new nations to dislike the United States. He wanted them to emulate it, and to aspire to be like it or even to be part of it. But these new republics were becoming de facto British commercial colonies. British trade in Latin America was double that of the United States there. Both the new nations and the United States were financially in debt to Britain. The U.S. government wanted to please Britain and to challenge it.

The proximate cause of the Monroe Doctrine could even be said to have been a British proposal for a joint doctrine, which the U.S. declined, preferring to make a statement on its own. British Foreign Secretary George Canning had written to U.S. Minister to Great Britain Richard Rush suggesting a joint U.S.-British declaration that none of the new nations could be transferred by Spain to any other power. Monroe wrote to Jefferson and Madison for advice, proposing that the United States should make it known "that we would view an interference on the part of the European powers, and especially an attack on the [South American] Colonies, by them, as an attack on ourselves."[69] This was a radically new proposal, a sort of proto-NATO membership for South America.

Jefferson told Monroe that this topic was the most important since independence, and that it was about "freedom," even while noting his desire to take over Cuba. In cabinet discussions, Secretary of War John C. Calhoun favored a joint statement with Britain even if it required committing not to take over Cuba or Texas. Monroe preferred to keep open the possibility of adding Cuba or Texas to the U.S. empire.[70] Some talked of a hemispheric empire. The *North American Review* in 1821 wrote, "South America will be to North America, we are strongly inclined to think, what Asia and Africa are to Europe."[71]

Historians tell us that the fear that the Holy Alliance would take over South American nations in 1823 was not actually remotely justified, and that (as we will see) this would be a pattern for the Monroe Doctrine; the British and French were not threatening anything when Polk used "Monroe's Doctrine" to steal half of Mexico; and Germany planned nothing when Theodore Roosevelt announced his Corollary.[72] Imagine how many claims not fully enshrined as "doctrines" have followed the pattern, from domino theories to missile gaps to weapons of mass destruction. Fear is such a powerful force that I feel obliged to now explicitly acknowledge the stupid point that sometimes threats are real. But rare is the war or military expansion not driven by unreal threats.

When Monroe made the speech that contained the doctrine, it was a speech packed with militarism and imperialism:

> *"The moneys appropriated for fortifications have been regularly and economically applied, and all the works advanced as rapidly as the amount appropriated would admit. . . . The Military Academy has attained a degree of perfection in its discipline and instruction equal, as is believed, to any institution of its kind in any country. . . . The fabrication of arms at the national armories and by contract with the Department has been gradually improving in quality and cheapness. . . . The completion of the fortifications renders it necessary that there should be a suitable appropriation for the purpose of fabricating the cannon and carriages necessary for those works. Under the appropriation of $5,000 for exploring the Western waters for the location of a site for a Western armory, a commission was constituted, ... During the month of June last General Ashley and his party, who were trading under a license from the Government, were attacked by the Ricarees while peaceably trading with the Indians at their request. . . . As the defense and even the liberties of the country must depend in times of imminent danger on the militia, it is of the highest importance that it be well organized, armed, and disciplined throughout the Union. . . . In*

the West Indies and the Gulf of Mexico our naval force has been augmented by the addition of several small vessels . . . . If we compare the present condition of our Union with its actual state at the close of our Revolution, the history of the world furnishes no example of a progress in improvement in all the important circumstances which constitute the happiness of a nation which bears any resemblance to it. At the first epoch our population did not exceed 3,000,000. By the last census it amounted to about 10,000,000, and, what is more extraordinary, it is almost altogether native, for the immigration from other countries has been inconsiderable. At the first epoch half the territory within our acknowledged limits was uninhabited and a wilderness. Since then new territory has been acquired of vast extent, comprising within it many rivers, particularly the Mississippi, the navigation of which to the ocean was of the highest importance to the original States. Over this territory our population has expanded in every direction, and new States have been established almost equal in number to those which formed the first bond of our Union. This expansion of our population and accession of new States to our Union have had the happiest effect on all its highest interests. That it has eminently augmented our resources and added to our strength and respectability as a power is admitted by all, but it is not in these important circumstances only that this happy effect is felt. It is manifest that by enlarging the basis of our system and increasing the number of States the system itself has been greatly strengthened in both its branches."

With ideas that owed much to John Quincy Adams, as well as to discussions with the whole cabinet, and advice from Jefferson and Madison, Monroe also stated the doctrine. Here it is again:

"The occasion has been judged proper for asserting, as a principle in which the rights and interests of the United States are involved,

that the American continents, by the free and independent condition which they have assumed and maintain, are henceforth not to be considered as subjects for future colonization by any European powers. . . .

"We owe it, therefore, to candor and to the amicable relations existing between the United States and those powers to declare that we should consider any attempt on their part to extend their system to any portion of this hemisphere as dangerous to our peace and safety. With the existing colonies or dependencies of any European power, we have not interfered and shall not interfere. But with the Governments who have declared their independence and maintained it, and whose independence we have, on great consideration and on just principles, acknowledged, we could not view any interposition for the purpose of oppressing them, or controlling in any other manner their destiny, by any European power in any other light than as the manifestation of an unfriendly disposition toward the United States."

This was an introduction of the idea of war into the questions of South America and Oregon. No government or even individual in either location had requested what Monroe was promising. It's not even clear that Monroe recognized anyone in either location as having the ability to request or refuse it.

While the words of the Monroe Doctrine would not be elevated to the status of a doctrine for years, they did not go unnoticed. Russia immediately declared them worthy of "the most profound contempt." Count Klemens von Metternich, Chancellor of the Austrian Empire, privately said that Monroe's statement was a "new act of revolt, more unprovoked, fully as audacious, and no less dangerous" than the American Revolution.[73] A British newspaper commented: "The plain Yankee of the matter is that the United States wish to monopolize to themselves the privilege of colonising

. . . every . . . part of the American Continent."[74] But another British paper applauded Monroe's speech as "directly British." Britain had already won from France a commitment not to intervene in Spanish America.[75]

Meanwhile, Latin American leaders generally praised Monroe's remarks, even while recognizing that Britain was the major power. But some managed to voice prescient suspicions. A Chilean businessman wrote: "But we have to be very careful: for the Americans of the north, the only Americans are themselves."[76]

Regardless of Monroe's speech, the United States did not bother to pursue good relations with the new American republics. The U.S. had few competent diplomats or even Spanish speakers and was geographically closer to England than to Argentina. The divide between monarchical Europe and democratic Americas was complicated by advances in freedom in Europe, and by monarchy and slavery in the Americas. But the tradition developed of labeling threats to empire or even to life as threats to "freedom."

Within South American nations themselves, elites sometimes aligned with European imperialists against popular demands, or aligned with the U.S. against Europeans or with Europeans against the United States. When Colombia and Brazil asked the U.S. government for a formal commitment to protect them militarily, they were refused. This was in an age when no president would have attempted such a thing without Congress, not even a president who had already suggested it in a speech.[77]

The speech did not immediately change international behavior. The U.S. and Britain went on both competing and collaborating. While the Holy Alliance had decided not to invade South America prior to the Monroe Doctrine, President Monroe reversed the actual chronology of events to falsely claim that his speech had kept them out.[78] One person who never fell for that claim was Simón Bolívar, who saw Britain, not the U.S., as the only important military and commercial power, and saw Britain's as the model government to be emulated.

Over a century later, President John F. Kennedy would remark in a speech in Dallas that he never gave because he was murdered earlier in the day, "It was not the Monroe Doctrine that kept all Europe away from this hemisphere - it was the strength of the British fleet and the width of the Atlantic Ocean."

Two years after the Monroe Doctrine was spoken, President John Quincy Adams sought to maintain Spanish rule over Cuba. When Bolívar invited the United States to an international congress in Panama, the debate in the U.S. Congress over the question of attending featured extensive racism toward South Americans (who would soon be frequently called South Americans, rather than residents of the one American continent). The debate also dragged on so long that when a delegation was finally approved and sent, it arrived too late to take part. The pro-slavery racists who opposed participation included Andrew Jackson, Martin Van Buren, James Polk, and John C. Calhoun, all of whom would play key roles in developing both the Democratic Party and the Monroe Doctrine.

Immediately after the Monroe Doctrine was spoken, U.S. military actions rolled on more or less as prior: [79]

1822-1825 Cuba (Spain
1824 Puerto Rico (Spain)
1827 Greece
1831-1832 Falkland Islands
1832 Sauk
1832 Sumatra
1833 Argentina

1835-1836 Peru

1835-1842 Seminole

1836 Mexico

1836-1837 Muskogee (Creek)

1838-1839 Sumatra

5. What Has Been Done with the Monroe Doctrine?

Two centuries of ever increasing militarism and secrecy is a massive topic. Even limiting the topic to the Western Hemisphere, I can provide here only the highlights, plus some themes, some examples, some lists and numbers, to hint at the full picture as far as I can make it out. It's a saga of military actions, including coups, and threats thereof, but also economic measures.

In 1829 Simón Bolívar wrote that the United States "seem destined to plague America to misery in the name of liberty."[80] Any widespread view of the United States as a potential protector in Latin America was very short-lived. According to a biographer of Bolívar, "There was a universal feeling in South America that this first-born republic, which ought to have helped the younger ones, was, on the contrary, only trying to encourage discord and to foment difficulties so as to intervene at the appropriate moment."[81]

The conquest of much of North America was the most dramatic implementation of the Monroe Doctrine, and the Monroe Doctrine was used as a justification for it, just as for interventions to the south. In fact, the Monroe Doctrine was first discussed under that name as justification for the U.S. war on Mexico that moved the western U.S. border south, swallowing up the present-day states of California, Nevada, and Utah, most of New Mexico, Arizona and Colorado, and parts of Texas, Oklahoma, Kansas, and Wyoming. By no means was that as far south as some would have liked to move the border.

The catastrophic war on the Philippines also grew out of a Monroe-Doctrine-justified war against Spain in the Caribbean. And global imperialism (as we will see) was a smooth expansion of the Monroe Doctrine.

But it is in reference to Latin America that the Monroe Doctrine is usually cited today, and the Monroe Doctrine has been central to a U.S. assault on its southern neighbors for 200 years. During these centuries, groups and individuals, including Latin American intellectuals, have both opposed the Monroe Doctrine's justification of imperialism and sought to argue that the Monroe Doctrine should be interpreted as promoting isolationism and multilateralism. Both approaches have had limited success. U.S. interventions have ebbed and flowed but never halted.

The popularity of the Monroe Doctrine as a reference point in U.S. discourse, which rose to amazing heights during the 19th century, practically achieving the status of the Declaration of Independence or Constitution, may in part be thanks to its lack of clarity and to its avoidance of committing the U.S. government to anything in particular, while sounding quite macho. As various eras added their "corollaries" and interpretations, commentators could defend their preferred version against others. But the dominant theme, both before and even more so after Theodore Roosevelt, has always been exceptionalist imperialism.

Monroe Doctrine

This is the mother of all doctrines, generally understood as telling European nations to stay out of the Western Hemisphere, but easily expanded to include sending the same message to China, and including various understandings of just how the United States should enforce it and why the United States is justified in doing so. The doctrines that follow are its children.

U.S. actions in Latin America have, through these two centuries, moved gradually through a number of overlapping periods in which first U.S. military interventions, then U.S.-supported coups, and finally U.S. financial and legal pressures reached their heights. There has been a fairly steady growth of U.S. economic investment and influence in Latin America from 1823 to the current day or at least close to the current day.

Following the age of revolutions, Spain maintained control only of Cuba and Puerto Rico. Spain tried to retake Mexico in 1829 and was defeated by Mexico with no help from the United States. In 1833, the British claimed the Falkland Islands, and the United States did nothing. President Andrew Jackson was focused on a genocide closer to home. For years, the French navy, with help from the British navy, blockaded Argentina, and the United States did nothing. In 1845, the British and French intervened in a dispute between Argentina and Uruguay, and the United States did nothing. These and other instances seemed to perfectly fit the prescription of the Monroe Doctrine, and U.S. inaction confirmed Latin American suspicions of the United States.

When the U.S. government did decide to act on the Monroe Doctrine outside of North America, it was also outside of the Western Hemisphere. In 1842, Daniel Webster warned Britain and France away from Hawaii.

Tyler Doctrine

This one is seldom included, perhaps because the Monroe Doctrine was not yet a common phrase, or because Hawaii is not exactly in the Western Hemisphere, or because -- Hawaii having later been made a state -- any imperialistic actions taken in relation to Hawaii in the past no longer exist. In any case, numerous sources refer to the Tyler Doctrine as the name for President John Tyler's Secretary of State Daniel Webster's instructions to Britain and France in 1842 to keep their hands off Hawaii.

When the U.S. decided to act closer to home, and to speak for the first time of "Monroe's Doctrine" as the justification, it was not to protect a neighbor from a European military. It was to attack and exploit the independent nation of Mexico, steal half its territory, and leave it so weak that a European nation would soon take its turn attacking.

As a Congressman in 1826, Polk had said that Monroe's words were "the mere expression of the opinion of the Executive . . . . The President had no power to bind the nation by such a pledge."[82] But in President Polk's 1845 State of the Union Address, Monroe's words are held up as a non-partisan or pre-partisan indisputable creed of Americanism. Polk focused in his speech on North America rather than all of the Americas, but made a more forceful statement about North America than Monroe had.[83] South America was of so little interest, that Polk could not be bothered to mention it, or to send a single representative to an 1847 hemispheric conference.

Polk edited out of his 1845 State of the Union a foreswearing of conquest that had been in a draft of the speech by George Bancroft, but Polk did not say that conquest was what he intended -- except in his diary where he noted that what he had in mind was taking California. Polk did claim that Texas was being added to the United States without violence, omitting the U.S.-backed war Texas had fought to secede from Mexico. Polk then claimed that Mexico was behaving in an inexplicably hostile manner toward the United States. He went on to denounce British claims in Oregon, explaining that "Oregon is a part of the North American continent, to which, it is confidently affirmed, the title of the United States is the best now in existence." Polk declared that "the United States, sincerely desirous of preserving relations of good understanding with all nations, can not in silence permit any European interference on the North American continent, and should any such interference be attempted will be ready to resist it at any and all hazards. . . . Near a quarter of a century ago the principle was distinctly announced to the world, in the annual message of one of my predecessors, that— 'The American continents, by the free and independent condition which they have assumed and maintain, are henceforth not to be considered as subjects for colonization by any European powers.'"

Polk would actually back off and compromise with the British on Oregon, but gin up a *casus belli* against Mexico. The U.S. war on liberal Mexico taught the rest of Latin America that democracy was weak. It led to not only a European intervention in Mexico (exactly what the Monroe Doctrine was supposedly aimed at preventing) but also a Civil War in the United States.

Following the 1846-1848 war, Polk wanted more, and went to Congress demanding that the United States take over Yucatán. Congress had had enough of Polk's lies and wars by then, did not believe his false claims that Europeans were preparing to attack Yucatán, and did not want more war just yet. But Polk's proposal to Congress allowed him to push a racist cops-of-the-world interpretation of the Monroe Doctrine, to be echoed later by Theodore Roosevelt. "Savage" Indians, Polk said, "were waging a war of extermination against the white race" in Yucatán, and the Monroe Doctrine gave the United States the unique right and responsibility to act.

Polk Doctrine

This is simply a restatement of the Monroe Doctrine, which is probably why it is not usually included in lists of doctrines. Or perhaps it is the Monroe Doctrine that should be renamed the Polk Doctrine, since it was Polk who made use of excerpts from an old speech by Monroe and treated them as a "doctrine."

Was the Monroe Doctrine a benign tool misused by Polk and his successors? The case for that would be stronger had the Monroe Doctrine ever been used benignly or had it been written in a manner to forestall imperialistic uses. But perhaps, after all, it was Polk who actually wrote the Monroe Doctrine by placing an old quotation in new speeches and explaining it as he saw fit. U.S. military actions to the south of the United States in the 1840s were as follows:

1842 Mexico
1844 Mexico
1846-1848 Mexico
1847-1850 Cayuse

That list does not include filibustering, meaning the adventuring of private groups of U.S. citizens taking it upon themselves to land in the Caribbean or Central America and declare themselves the rulers of all they surveyed. Many of these escapades failed, and many were mocked, but others celebrated, in the U.S. media. But there was a great deal of support for them in the U.S. government, in the U.S. business world, and in the record of how the continental United States had been conquered and how it was still being conquered in places like Oregon. What was Texas, after all, if not successful filibustering. Why couldn't the same be done in Cuba? Many a filibustering fiasco in Cuba long preceded the Bay of Pigs SNAFU.

In 1853, newspapers first widely used the phrase "Monroe Doctrine" when the U.S. Senate considered a resolution on it, sponsored by Senator Lewis Cass. On January 20, 1853, the *New York Times* professed great admiration for a speech on the topic by Cass.[84] On February 14, 1853, Senator Stephen Douglas gave a speech in which he pointed out that it had become customary to profess support for the Monroe Doctrine but never to act in accordance with it. Douglas expressed his concern that Cass's resolution might be read as approving of any European colonies already established, including British claims to islands off Honduras or part of Nicaragua. The resolution, which was never put to a vote, specifically referred to Cuba, claiming that the United States would not try to seize Cuba but would view efforts by any European power (other than Spain) to do so as "unfriendly acts . . . to be resisted by all the means in [the United States'] power."[85]

Douglas became the leading proponent of Monroe-Doctrine-justified imperialism, telling Abraham Lincoln in their debates that imperialism was more important than ending slavery. Douglas wanted a white-supremacist imperial United States that would include all of North (and Central) America. He wanted no compromises with Britain.

At this point in U.S. history few issues were separable from divisions and debates over slavery. A compromise with Britain over Oregon was not only a compromise with the world's biggest navy but also over territory with the potential to add free states to the United States. Texas and Cuba meanwhile seemed not only easier to obtain, but to have the potential to expand U.S. lands for slavery. When the United States forced Mexico to give up its northern territories, U.S. diplomat Nicholas Trist negotiated most firmly on one point. He wrote to the U.S. Secretary of State: "I assured [the Mexicans] that if it were in their power to offer me the whole territory described in our project, increased ten-fold in value, and, in addition to that, covered a foot thick all over with pure gold, upon the single condition that slavery should be excluded therefrom, I could not entertain the offer for a moment."

But the whole world was banning slavery, including in Latin America. Slavery needed U.S. expansion. At one point Texas and Britain had considered joining together, and John Quincy Adams had wanted Britain to ban slavery in Texas. But, of course, Texas had violently seceded from Mexico in order to keep slavery. Joining the United States best served that cause of "freedom." And from the perspective of U.S. politicians, such as John C. Calhoun, who favored slavery, adding more territories served multiple purposes. Not only would it balance or outweigh the power of the free states in Washington, D.C., but it would add fresh soil to an enterprise that was only profitable on a large scale on fresh earth, an enterprise that regularly destroyed croplands through intensive one-crop farming. In addition, a slave society needs new places for the children of slaveowners to own more slaves in, and can sustain the areas depleted of fertile soil only by using them to raise slaves for sale to the regions not yet ruined.

Abolitionists long understood the need for slavery to expand and sought to prevent its expansion -- a strategy weakened by their own unquestioning support for the general expansion of the United States.

The Whigs played the role of the party partially and fecklessly opposed to excessive imperialism, even while finding it obligatory to interpret the Monroe Doctrine to mean what each of them wanted it to mean. Whig Senator and future Secretary of State William Henry Seward favored expansion, just not of slavery. He thought cooperation with Britain was compatible with the Monroe Doctrine. He foresaw the joining of nations into a U.S.-dominated international congress and free-trade agreement, and the primary purpose of the United States as winning the international competition for commercial dominance.

The Monroe Doctrine was the one thing U.S. politicians agreed on, though they disagreed on what it meant. They could avoid the slavery debate, if they chose, by discussing who was more patriotic than whom, who was a greater champion of the Monroe Doctrine. Yet the imperialism of the Monroe Doctrine debates intensified the division over slavery, as the sides could not agree on whether to attack Cuba or on how to add portions of the West to the nation.

U.S. military actions in the Western Hemisphere in the 1850s (not counting filibusterers) included:

1850-1886 Apache
1852-1853 Argentina
1853-1854 Nicaragua
1855 Uruguay
1855-1856 Rogue River Indigenous Peoples
1855-1856 Yakima, Walla Walla, Cayuse
1855-1858 Seminole

1856 Panama (Colombia)
1857 Nicaragua
1858 Coeur d'Alene Alliance
1858 Uruguay
1859 Mexico
1859 Paraguay

In 1848, Nicaragua actually asked the U.S. government for protection against the British, and the U.S. government did nothing. The topic of greatest interest to the U.S. in Latin America for many years was, not the need to protect any struggling young republic from invading monarchies, but the possibility of building and owning and controlling a canal to connect the Atlantic and Pacific oceans. Interest in this long-standing goal surged when the gold rush to California took off in 1849. In 1850, the U.S. and Britain made an agreement with each other about the use of Nicaragua for a canal, without consulting Nicaragua. They called the agreement the Clayton-Bulwer Treaty -- John M. Clayton being a U.S. Secretary of State who, according to the British, informed the British that the U.S. did not really abide by the Monroe Doctrine.[86]

Britain maintained a colony, or perhaps it should be called a proxy state, on the Mosquito Coast of Nicaragua, a likely location for one end of a canal. For years, the United States warned Britain of the requirements of the Monroe Doctrine, which merely seemed to annoy the Brits, until finally in 1860 Britain decided that it preferred for the U.S. to control Nicaragua, and picked up and left.

Meanwhile, the lack of a canal wasn't stopping the North Americans from sailing to Nicaragua and traveling across it, to sail the second half of the journey to California from the other coast. Some even stopped in Nicaragua to build hotels and otherwise profit from the through traffic. U.S. chargé d'affaires Ephraim G. Squier reported that not everyone in

Nicaragua was completely happy with the arrival of the gringos, because the North Americans shot at Indians along the banks of the San Juan River for target practice.[87] I suppose that's one way to mentor people in the ways of democracy.

The United States had also begun the practice of sending in the Marines to take over territories for the interests of U.S. companies. In 1853, Cornelius Vanderbilt's Accessory Transit Company erected buildings without permission, and the city of San Juan decided to tear them down. In came the Marine Corps to make sure Vanderbilt's company could violate laws it chose to violate. This was the first of countless such actions in Nicaragua and elsewhere. In July of 1854 Nicaraguans sought to arrest a U.S. captain for murder. U.S. Minister Solon Borland, who liked to lecture Nicaragua on the Monroe Doctrine and who was highly offended by the mixing of races permitted in Nicaragua, put a stop to the pursuit of the murderer but got a bottle thrown at him. When no apology was forthcoming for the bottle throwing, the U.S. bombarded the city and sent in the Marines to loot and pillage, get drunk on stolen liquor, and burn the buildings down.[88] Huge volumes could be filled with accounts of such incidents throughout Latin America, as well as pretty much everywhere that has been militarily occupied by another country throughout world history.

Eventually, of course, the canal would end up in Panama. Between 1856 and 1903, the United States would intervene in Panama at least 13 times, with more to come in the years that followed.

When it comes to the escapades of arrogant gringos, no sampling of tales would be complete without the somewhat unique but revealing story of William Walker, a filibusterer who made himself president of Nicaragua, carrying south the expansion that predecessors like Daniel Boone had carried west. Walker is not secret CIA history. The CIA had yet to exist. During the 1850s Walker may have received more attention in

U.S. newspapers than any U.S. president. On four different days, the *New York Times* devoted its entire front page to his antics. That most people in Central America know his name and virtually nobody in the United States does is a choice made by the respective educational systems.

In 1853, doctor/lawyer/journalist/jack-of-all-trades William Walker gathered a group together and appealed to the government of Mexico to allow them to colonize Sonora. But Mexico had learned its lesson with Texas and refused. So Walker simply sailed his gang down to Baja California and declared it the "Republic of Lower California," later claiming Sonora as well, without setting foot in it. But the U.S. government purchased a chunk of Sonora called the Gadsden Purchase, and cut off Walker's supply of recruits from California. However, U.S. Secretary of War and future President of the Confederacy Jefferson Davis made sure Walker was not punished. The U.S. government saw Walker as helpful to its negotiating the purchase of land from Mexico that the Mexicans would know they might simply lose if they didn't sell. And slavery promoters viewed the Gadsden Purchase as key to expanding slavery.

Next Walker got himself the command of a North American force supposedly aiding one of two warring parties in Nicaragua, but actually doing what Walker chose, which included capturing the city of Granada, effectively taking charge of the country, and eventually holding a phony election of himself. Walker got to work transferring land ownership to gringos, instituting slavery, and making English an official language. Newspapers in the southern U.S. wrote about Nicaragua as a future U.S. state. But Walker managed to make an enemy of Vanderbilt, and to unite Central America as never before, across political divisions and national borders, against him. Only the U.S. government professed "neutrality." Defeated, Walker was welcomed back to the United States as a conquering hero. He tried again in Honduras in 1860 and ended up captured by the British, turned over to Honduras, and shot by a firing squad. His soldiers were sent back to the United States where they mostly joined the Confederate Army.

Walker had preached the gospel of war. "They are but drivellers," he said, "who speak of establishing fixed relations between the pure white American race, as it exists in the United States, and the mixed, Hispano-Indian race, as it exists in Mexico and Central America, without the employment of force." Walker's vision was adored and celebrated by U.S. media, not to mention a Broadway show.[89]

During the U.S. Civil War, both sides hoped, after victory, to use the Monroe Doctrine to expand their glorious empire, respectively slave or free, to the south. For Northerners, the secession of the South, combined with Southern appeals for British intervention -- plus some Southerners wanting France back in Haiti -- was like the fulfillment of longstanding nightmarish fears of internal division and European intervention. But when the North threatened war on Britain, Britain told the South it would not join the war, that it would in fact abide by the Monroe Doctrine (at least in this instance).

The U.S. Civil War, and the recent expulsion of filibusterers, provided some relief to countries like Nicaragua. In Nicaragua, a period of 36 years began in 1857 that is considered a time of relative peace and stability.

A major test of the Monroe Doctrine came in Mexico in 1861. With the United States busy attacking itself in civil war, British, French, and Spanish ships all showed up in Mexico demanding debt payments. They had invited the United States to join them; it had declined but also not opposed. U.S. Minister to Mexico Thomas Corwin proposed a U.S. loan to Mexico with which, effectively, to pay Europe to abide by the Monroe Doctrine, while locking Mexico in to extensive trade with the United States and demanding mineral-rich lands as collateral. The U.S. Senate never ratified

Corwin's treaty, but it pointed a way forward for the U.S. government in Latin America and elsewhere. The Mexican government, and other Latin American governments, were very open to accepting economic support, even with strings attached.

Only the French stayed long in Mexico. They intended to impose a puppet monarchy, and did just that in early 1864, making Austrian Archduke Ferdinand Maximilian Josef Maria von Habsburg-Lothringen the Emperor of Mexico. The U.S. South hoped for French support, while the North tended to view the French assault on Mexico as a conspiracy with the Confederacy. Many Republicans, even Francis Lieber, of the famous Lieber Code for proper war conduct, thought the United States would need to intervene in Mexico. The Mexican Minister to the United States invoked the Monroe Doctrine repeatedly. Following the U.S. Civil War, the United States began sending aid to republican forces in Mexico. In 1866 French armies began withdrawing. They had another war to fight in Europe. Ulysses S. Grant put U.S. troops on the Mexican border and urged President Andrew Johnson to order an invasion. In 1867 the French cleared out and the monarchy fell. According to Jay Sexton, the Monroe Doctrine had played a minor role:

> *"[M]ost Americans inflated their own role in ending the French intervention in Mexico. Never mind the blood and treasure expended by the Mexican resistance; never mind that the British and Spanish abandoned the intervention in Mexico; never mind the important role played by critics of Napoleon in France, who campaigned against the venture. Americans concluded that it was their Monroe Doctrine that prompted France's ignominious withdrawal from Mexico. In the coming decades, politicians would state this as truth, schoolbooks would teach it, and Americans would internalize it."*[90]

While it seems false that the Monroe Doctrine (and related U.S. actions) was the only factor, it also seems highly unlikely that it was no factor at all. When the U.S. was tied up with its civil war, Spain also tried to retake the Dominican Republic, but abandoned it upon the completion of the U.S. Civil War. Also during the U.S. Civil War, Spain occupied the Chincha Islands off the coast of Peru. They were full of the valuable fertilizer that was bird or bat poop, known as guano. Grabbing such islands was standard practice. The United States itself had passed the Guano Islands Act in 1856, essentially applying the Doctrine of Discovery to any unclaimed island with guano on it. The U.S. claimed 94 guano islands between 1857 and 1900, used slave labor to scrape up the guano and ship it to the imperial mainland, and repeatedly threatened or risked or backed off from war over the stuff, rather than ever facing the fact that only sustainable farming would have been a lasting solution to its destruction of its own land. Also during the U.S. Civil War, the British consolidated their colonies in today's Belize and called them British Honduras. The United States did nothing.

Meanwhile, Paraguay had become, under a brutal dictatorship, the only Latin American country not dependent on foreign trade and investment, the only country with complete literacy, the only country without hunger, begging, or stealing. Paraguay had telegraphs, a railroad, and all kinds of factories. Britain was not pleased. Britain's Minister to Buenos Aires Edward Thornton worked to organize a joint-operation genocide, to be committed by Argentina, Brazil, and Uruguay against Paraguay from 1865 to 1870, paid for by the Bank of London, Baring Brothers, and the Rothschild Bank, with the loot ending up in British pockets. Only one-sixth of the Paraguayan population survived. Recounts Eduardo Galeano:

> *"In defeated Paraguay, it was not only the population and great chunks of territory that disappeared, but customs tariffs, foundries, rivers closed to free trade, and economic independence. Within its shrunken frontiers, the conquerors implanted free trade and the latifundio. Everything was looted and everything was sold: land and*

forests, mines, verba maté farms, school buildings. Successive puppet governments were installed in Asunción by the occupation forces. The war was hardly over when the first foreign loan in Paraguay's history fell upon the smoking ruins. It was, of course, British."[91]

The imposition on Latin America of financial control, and the maintenance of governments that have been, to one degree or another, puppets is an endless story of which this is but one incident. But each incident has sent ripples down to the present day. The United States, of course, did nothing to protect Uruguay, and when Lyndon Johnson restated the Monroe-Kennedy Doctrine while attacking the Dominican Republic, some Paraguayan (as well as Nicaraguan) soldiers helped him, under the direction of the Brazilian military. Paraguay also gave Brazil oil, although Brazil's oil business was in U.S. hands. Paraguay became indebted to New York banks. Paraguay has never recovered.

In the 1860s the United States continued to reject invitations to join in meetings of Latin American nations, preferring to stay on better terms with European powers. U.S. discussions of the Monroe Doctrine continued to increase and to be made ever more racist, exceptionalist, and imperialist. U.S. military actions in the Western Hemisphere in the 1860s included:

1860 Colombia
1862 Sioux
1864 Cheyenne
1865 Panama (Colombia)
1866 Mexico
1866-1868 Lakota Sioux, Northern Cheyenne, Northern Arapaho
1867 Nicaragua
1867-1875 Comanche
1868 Colombia
1868 Uruguay

Most U.S. military attacks abroad in the 1870s were against Native American nations of North America. During the second half of the nineteenth century, the United States would largely complete the takeover of its continental mainland. Meanwhile, canal dreams continued, as they would for decades. Secretary of State Hamilton Fish developed what Karl Bermann called the Fish Corollary to the Monroe Doctrine, when he told the U.S. Minister to Nicaragua not to let any nation other than the United States get access to build a canal.[92]

Fish Corollary

This is a rarely mentioned one. In 1871, U.S. Secretary of State Hamilton Fish told his subordinate to make sure that Nicaragua did not allow any other country any authority to build a canal between the Atlantic and Pacific until the United States had decided whether it wanted to do it.

The U.S. would go on intervening during the 1870s in Colombia and Mexico. Colombia, from which the U.S. would break off Panama, was a potential canal site. In 1870, President Grant also proposed taking over the Dominican Republic for purposes of guarding the not-yet-existing canal. Grant also hoped that people freed from slavery by the U.S. Civil War would get the heck out of the country and perhaps relocate to the Dominican Republic. Grant had no trouble getting the Dominican government to agree to a U.S. takeover, but did have trouble with the U.S. Congress. Grant tried citing the Monroe Doctrine and pretending that some European power might soon take over the Dominican Republic if the U.S. didn't, but his plan was still voted down.

Secretary of State Fish had subtler schemes. Rather than invasions, Fish plotted and argued for informal imperialism: establishing protectorates, acquiring new markets, and imposing advantageous trade agreements. In the long run, such schemes have probably killed more people than wars have, but Fish's aversion to wars did some good as well. When, in 1872,

Spain seemed set on war with Bolivia, Chile, Ecuador, and Peru, Fish invited them all to a negotiating table in Washington, D.C., and made peace. This seems to be a rare instance of the Monroe Doctrine being used accurately and in a beneficial manner for a beneficial purpose. If only lessons had been learned!

Another expansionist approach was still the financial purchase. In 1867, the United States bought Alaska from Russia.

U.S. military actions in the Western Hemisphere in the 1870s included:

1872-1873 Modoc
1873 Colombia (Panama)
1873-1896 Mexico
1874-1875 Comanche, Apache, Arapaho, Cheyenne, Kiowa
1876-1877 Sioux
1877 Nez Perce
1878 Bannock (Banna'kwut)
1878-1879 Cheyenne
1879-1880 Utes

In 1881 U.S. Secretary of State James G. Blaine created what might be (but as far as I know hasn't been) called the Blaine Doctrine or Blaine Corollary, when he told the U.S. Minister to England that the U.S. was claiming the right to ignore the Clayton-Bulwer Treaty and make its own canal as it damn well liked. Blaine pointed out that only the United States was capable of ensuring the neutrality of the canal, which, he explained, would mean that U.S. war ships would always have access to the canal while other nations' ships would only have such access in peacetime. Blaine argued for this on the grounds that Great Britain had a right to the Suez Canal because it needed it for its large navy and because of the locations of its imperial possessions. Similarly, Blaine said, the United States would always need a Central American canal and "insist upon treating [it] as part of her coast-line."[93]

Not only did Blaine anticipate Orwell by formulating a definition of "neutrality" in which some are more equal than others, but he also announced what he called a "Big Brother Policy." This was to be a sort of free trade agreement with some more free than others. Blaine revived a long-proposed but never acted-on idea for a Pan-American Conference and sought to create it for years, before finally doing so in 1889 during his second stint as Secretary of State. The United States had skipped out on, been uninvited, or made little of four hemispheric conferences between 1826 and 1864, but this was a U.S.-initiated conference. It accomplished little, but several more would follow over the decades. It did form a predecessor to the Organization of American States (OAS) which would be formed at a similar conference in 1948.

Blaine had had hopes for an Inter-American bank, a Texas to Chile railroad, and steamships up and down the globe. He also had hopes for arbitration as a sensible alternative to war. But when Blaine fell ill, and a dispute arose with Chile, U.S. President Benjamin Harrison's approach was to disregard arbitration and threaten Chile. There was, in fact, little support in the U.S. government for engagement with Latin America on anything even resembling equal terms. Blain's conference seems to have conveyed a fairly positive message to some, that was simply not followed through on. But we should not overestimate how fair a message was ever intended, or how many people ever heard it in a positive way.

In the lead-up to the conference, Cuban writer José Martí had written in a Buenos Aires newspaper denouncing the Monroe Doctrine as hypocrisy and accusing the United States of invoking "freedom . . . for purposes of depriving other nations of it." Martí sarcastically claimed that the United States had never caused any trouble at all for Latin American countries:

> *"This powerful neighbor has never desired to incite them, nor has it exerted control over them except to prevent their expansion, as in Panama; or to take possession of their territory, as in Mexico, Nicaragua, Santo Domingo, Haiti, and Cuba; or to cut off their trade with the rest of the world, as in Colombia; or to oblige them to buy what it cannot sell, as it is now doing, and to form a confederacy for the purpose of controlling them."*

Martí pointed out that the U.S. government had sent Frederick Douglas to Haiti in hopes of negotiating a U.S. military base there and perhaps a protectorate of the whole nation, that the U.S. was trying to negotiate Cuba away from Spain, that the U.S. had been stirring up trouble against Mexico in Costa Rica and Colombia, that U.S. companies were taking over Honduras, that the U.S. Congress hoped to make Nicaragua a state, that a U.S. newspaper in advocating for the purchase of Alaska had proclaimed a vision of the U.S. flag flying from the icy North to the Isthmus and ocean to ocean.

Martí chronicled the recent outrages and future schemes:

> *"Walker went to Nicaragua for the United States; for the United States [another filibusterer] Lopez went to Cuba. And now when slavery is no longer an excuse, the annexation alliance is afoot. Allen is talking about helping that of Cuba; Douglass is going to obtain that of Haiti and Santo Domingo. In Madrid Palmer is gauging Spain's feelings about the sale of Cuba; in the Antilles the bribed Central American newspapers are stirring up interest in the Washington-based annexation plans; in the lesser Antilles the Northern newspapers are constantly giving reports on the progress of annexationist ideas. Washington persists in compelling Colombia to acknowledge its dictatorial rights over the isthmus, and in depriving it of the authority to discuss its territory with other nations. And the*

United States, by virtue of the civil war it instigated, is acquiring the Mole St. Nicolas peninsula in Haiti."[94]

In reality, Douglass never persuaded Haiti to give the U.S. a base, after the U.S. Navy showed up in Haiti with war ships, angering the Haitians. But that didn't mean that the U.S. would ever leave Haiti in peace.

U.S. military actions in the Western Hemisphere in the 1880s included:

1885 Panama (Colombia)
1888 Haiti

U.S. imperialism rolled right along through the 1890s, right up to the date when we're traditionally told it first began, 1898.

An incident occurred in 1895 that impacted the use of the Monroe Doctrine. A longstanding border dispute between Venezuela and Britain -- that is Venezuela and British Guiana -- was made into a major matter in Washington D.C. when Venezuela learned a trick that many governments would practice in the decades to come. Unable to get a response out of the U.S. government, Venezuela resorted to hiring a former U.S. official to lobby for it.

William Lindsay Scruggs was a former U.S. ambassador. He argued, on behalf of Venezuela, that Britain was in violation of the Monroe Doctrine. That the Monroe Doctrine was just some words scattered through an old speech was the furthest thing from a response the U.S. government would have dreamed of making. Scruggs successfully urged both houses of Congress to unanimously pass and President Grover Cleveland to sign a resolution stating that Venezuela and the United Kingdom should settle the dispute by arbitration.

Secretary of State Richard Olney then sent to London a 12,000 word note claiming that the Monroe Doctrine meant the United States needed to be listened to: "[T]oday the United States is practically sovereign on this continent, and its fiat is law upon the subjects to which it confines its interposition." The British were not impressed. They argued such points as that the current situation was different from what James Monroe had been speaking about, as well as the obvious point that international law cannot be made by a president's speech. President Cleveland then made a vaguely bellicose speech to Congress and asked the Congress to fund a study of the dispute, which it did.

In the end, the British tacitly recognized the U.S. right, under the Monroe Doctrine, to intervene, and submitted to arbitration. The arbitration was to be done by a commission made up of two members representing Venezuela but chosen by the U.S., two members chosen by the British government, and a fifth member chosen by those four. Venezuela objected, rather understandably, that Britain got to pick two members and it did not get to pick any. The agreement was modified, so that Venezuela could choose one member, but it was understood that the choice would not be of a Venezuelan -- that would have just been going too far. In the end, two Brits and two U.S. members chose a Russian diplomat as the fifth. In 1899 a decision was reached, with no explanation, and highly favorable to Britain.

While Venezuela had lost the dispute, the British and the U.S. seemed to believe that it was Britain that had really lost in a rivalry with the up-and-coming U.S. empire. In part this was because Cleveland's speech had been heard in the United States as a call to war, and the usual madness of war fever had kicked in.

In his speech, Cleveland claimed that "the [Monroe] doctrine upon which we stand is strong and sound, because its enforcement is important to our peace and safety as a nation and is essential to the integrity of our free institutions and the tranquil maintenance of our distinctive form of government." In this we see that the Monroe Doctrine was not to be simply about protecting other nations, but to somehow be a matter of self-defense and preservation of the form of the U.S. government. In this, Cleveland was drawing on the words "dangerous to our peace and safety" in the doctrine itself. The doctrine was also to be permanent:

> *"It was intended to apply to every stage of our national life and can not become obsolete while our Republic endures. If the balance of power is justly a cause for jealous anxiety among the Governments of the Old World and a subject for our absolute noninterference, none the less is an observance of the Monroe doctrine of vital concern to our people and their Government."*

Cleveland replied to the British complaint that a U.S. president cannot simply invent international law by effectively claiming that oh yes he can.[95]

Olney Corollary

This is another lesser, or rarely mentioned, doctrine. The Olney Corollary or Interpretation or Declaration refers to the 1895 claim by U.S. Secretary of State Richard Olney that the U.S. government could compel other governments engaged in a dispute in the Western Hemisphere to submit to arbitration.

In 1898, the Monroe Doctrine was used to help launch the Spanish-American war, but so was a flood of almost modern propaganda, demonizing Spain, and blaming Spain for a supposed attack that had killed U.S. sailors -- to whom there are still monuments around the United States to this day. A U.S. ship, the *USS Maine*, the mast from which is on display at the U.S. Naval Academy, blew up in Havana Harbor, and U.S. newspapers quickly blamed the Spanish, crying out "Remember the Maine! To hell with Spain!" Newspaper owner William Randolph Hearst did his best to fan the flames of a war he knew would boost circulation.

Who actually blew the ship up? Nobody knew. Certainly Spain denied it, Cuba denied it, and the United States denied it. Spain didn't just casually deny it either. Spain conducted an investigation and found that the explosion had been inside the ship. Realizing that the United States would reject this finding, Spain proposed a joint investigation by both countries and offered to submit to binding arbitration by an impartial international panel -- not unlike what the United States had just compelled Britain and Venezuela to submit to. But the U.S. government refused. Whatever caused the explosion, Washington wanted war.

More recent investigations raise the distinct possibility that the Maine was indeed sunk by an explosion, whether accidental or intentional, that occurred within it, rather than by a mine outside it. But no experts have proven one theory over another to the satisfaction of all, and I'm not sure what good it would do. The Spanish could have found a way to plant a bomb inside the ship. Americans could have found a way to place a mine outside it. Knowing where the explosion took place won't tell us who, if anyone, caused it. But even if we knew for certain who caused it, how, and why, none of that information would change the basic account of what happened in 1898.

This is what happened. The United States went mad for war in response to an attack by Spain for which there was no evidence, merely conjecture. A U.S. ship had blown up, Americans had been killed, and there was a possibility that Spain might be responsible. In combination with other grievances against Spain, this was excuse enough to bang the war drums. The pretense of certainty that Spain was to blame was nothing other than a pretense. This alleged atrocity was used to launch a war "in defense of" Cuba and the Philippines that involved attacking and occupying Cuba and the Philippines, and Puerto Rico for good measure.

Cuba was fighting Spain for its independence. It would end up under U.S. occupation. So would the Philippines, Guam, and Puerto Rico. The Spanish-American War was not fought in Spain or the United States. It was fought in Cuba, Puerto Rico, Guam, and the Philippines. The United States saw 496 killed in action, 202 died of wounds, 5,509 died from disease, and 250 were killed very likely by the United States' own, presumably accidental, destruction of the *USS Maine* prior to the war. The Spanish saw 786 killed in action, 8,627 died of wounds, and 53,440 died from disease. The Cubans saw another 10,665 dead.[96]

But it was in the Philippines that the death count, as well as the length of the war (1899 to 1913), took on a shape familiar to 21st century eyes. The United States had 4,000 killed, mostly by disease, plus 64 from Oregon. The Philippines had 20,000 combatants killed, plus 200,000 to 1,500,000 civilians dead from violence and diseases, including cholera. By some estimates, the United States' occupying forces, together with disease, killed over 1.5 million civilians in the Philippines, out of a population of 6 to 7 million -- 21% of the population. If that high estimate is right, then, second to the genocidal attacks on Native American nations, this war was, by this measure, the worst war the United States has ever engaged in.[97]

In 1899 a global peace conference was held in The Hague, Netherlands. Since that date (except as updated by a newer treaty in 1907), all parties to the Convention for the Pacific Settlement of International Disputes have committed that they "agree to use their best efforts to insure the pacific settlement of international differences."[98] Violation of this treaty would, in 1945, become the first charge in the Nuremberg Indictment of Nazis. Parties to the convention have, since 1899, included enough nations to effectively eliminate war if it were complied with. The United States participated in the conference, and signed and ratified the treaty, just one year after going to enormous lengths to avoid peace with Spain. But the U.S. submitted this "reservation" to its compliance with the treaty:

> *"While signing the Convention for the Pacific Settlement of International Disputes in the form proposed by the International Peace Conference, the delegation of the United States of America makes the following Declaration: Nothing contained in the Convention may be interpreted as obliging the United States of America to deviate from its traditional policy of abstaining from intervention, interference and intrusion in the political questions or in the policy or in the domestic administration of any foreign state. It is likewise understood that nothing in the Convention shall be interpreted as implying the abandonment by the United States of America of its traditional attitude in respect of purely American questions."*[99]

In other words, the U.S. would join the world of international law, and move beyond the age of settling disputes with mass killing, unless doing so conflicted with the Monroe Doctrine. When Olney proposed a future system of arbitration for disputes between the U.S. and the UK, the U.S. Senate rejected that as well.

While it's important not to believe that U.S. imperialism began in 1898, how people in the United States thought of U.S. imperialism did change in 1898 and the years following. There were now greater bodies of water between the mainland and its colonies and possessions. There were greater numbers of people not deemed "white" living below U.S. flags. And there was apparently no longer a need to respect the rest of the hemisphere by understanding the name "America" to apply to more than one nation. Up until this time, the United States of America was usually refered to as the United States or the Union. Now it became America. So, if you thought your little country was in America, you'd better watch out![100]

U.S. military actions in the Western Hemisphere in the 1890s included:

1890 Argentina
1890 Lakota Sioux
1891 Bering Strait
1891 Chile
1891 Haiti
1894 Brazil
1894 Nicaragua
1895 Panama (Colombia)
1896 Nicaragua
1898 Cuba (Spain)
1898 Nicaragua
1898 Puerto Rico (Spain)
1899 Nicaragua

With the opening of the 20th century, the United States fought fewer battles in North America, but more in South and Central America. The mythical idea that a larger military prevents wars, rather than instigates them, often looks back to Theodore Roosevelt claiming that the United States would speak softly but carry a big stick -- something that Vice President Roosevelt cited as an African proverb in a speech in 1901, four days before President William McKinley was killed, making Roosevelt president.

While it may be pleasant to imagine Roosevelt preventing wars by threatening with his stick, the reality is that he used the U.S. military for more than just show in Panama in 1901, Colombia in 1902, Honduras in 1903, the Dominican Republic in 1903, Syria in 1903, Abyssinia in 1903, Panama in 1903, the Dominican Republic in 1904, Morocco in 1904, Panama in 1904, Korea in 1904, Cuba in 1906, Honduras in 1907, and the Philippines throughout his presidency.

The century opened with Cuba under U.S. military occupation, following a war supposedly fought for Cuban independence. The Cubans were never going to stand for annexation by the United States. (Also, the United States was never going to give back its base at Guantanamo.) The U.S. looked to Britain's example of maintaining rights in Egypt after leaving it. The Platt Amendment to a U.S. military appropriations bill restricted Cuba's independence and its ability to borrow money, ceded Guantanamo to the United States, and gave the U.S. the explicit right to "intervene" when it saw fit. Secretary of War Elihu Root sold the Platt Amendment to the U.S. public as an action in compliance with the Monroe Doctrine, even though no European nation was threatening anything in Cuba, and imposing U.S. rule on Cuba did not make Cuba independent.

Meanwhile the U.S. forced Britain to abandon the Clayton-Bulwer Treaty by creating the Hay-Pauncefote Treaty of 1901, allowing the U.S. to build and control a canal in Panama on its own and to fortify it. When Colombia wouldn't immediately agree to U.S. terms, Roosevelt gave military support to Panamanian rebels. By 1903, the new nation of Panama had been taken from Colombia, and within two weeks, Panama had given land for a canal to the United States; before long, the United Fruit Company (now Chiquita) would become dominant in Panama, as also in the banana republics of Costa Rica, Honduras, and Guatemala.

At the same time, Roosevelt and others in Washington were dramatically exaggerating a supposed German threat to the Western Hemisphere and the Monroe Doctrine, which German Chancellor Otto von Bismarck called a "special manifestation of American arrogance."

While smaller-scale military actions were on the rise, the trends were against major wars, and against attempts at outright acquisition, in favor of more hidden controls, the imposition of laws and treaties, and the economic dominance of business monopolies with close ties to the U.S. government. At the same time, the language of imperialism was more acceptable than ever, and it was in 1904 that President Theodore Roosevelt announced his famous "Roosevelt Corollary" to the Monroe Doctrine. Today, if you learn about the Monroe Doctrine in U.S. public schools, you are likely to learn that it was a kind and friendly decree that nothing much was done with until Teddy Roosevelt turned it upside down. The problem with that tall tale is everything mentioned thus far in this book -- plus mountains more as I am providing only highlights and examples.

The Roosevelt Corollary included these words: "Chronic wrongdoing, or an impotence which results in a general loosening of the ties of civilized society, may in America, as elsewhere, ultimately require intervention by some civilized nation, and in the Western Hemisphere the adherence of the United States to the Monroe Doctrine may force the United States, however reluctantly, in flagrant cases of such wrongdoing or impotence, to the exercise of an international police power." Roosevelt was claiming a license for wars, whether or not any claim to U.S. self-defense could be made, whether or not any claim to defending U.S. "interests" could be made, and whether or not the wars took place in the Western Hemisphere. He quickly used this claim to justify numerous interventions in Latin America.

The Roosevelt Corollary was not only a friendly amendment to the Monroe Doctrine, but it also arose out of public demand for upholding the Monroe Doctrine. In 1902, the U.S. had given its blessing to German and British gunboat-diplomacy debt-collection in Venezuela. But when the gunboats began sinking ships and firing on land, the U.S. began to view the matter as a violation of the Monroe Doctrine. Roosevelt urged the parties to take the matter to the Hague arbitration tribunal, which ruled in favor of the nations with the gunboats.

At the same time, in Santo Domingo (the Dominican Republic) the nation was in debt to both the United States and European powers, the latter were threatening to attack, and the government appealed to Roosevelt to uphold the Monroe Doctrine. It was at this point that Roosevelt stood up, thumped his chest, and announced his Corollary. Jay Sexton points out one of many alternative courses of action that were available. Argentine Foreign Minister Luis María Drago had proposed that all the nations of the Western Hemisphere jointly announce an expansion of the Monroe Doctrine to include opposition to any and all interventions aimed at collecting debts. This Drago Doctrine might have been enshrined as a holy duty of U.S. foreign policy if foreigners were allowed to have doctrines, if the U.S. government were willing to be one among equals, and if the U.S. had been willing to give up its own military actions in order to have Europe do the same.[101]

Drago may have been trying to alter the Monroe Doctrine while claiming to extend it, but that was a common pastime of U.S. politicians as well. Canada for its part, in 1902, in the person of Prime Minister Wilfrid Laurier, expressed support for the Monroe Doctrine as protection of Canada. This was in line with Theodore Roosevelt's expansion of the Monroe Doctrine into a decree from (to use the title of a Phill Ochs song from some sixty years later) the Cops of the World:

We've rammed in your harbor and tied to your port
And our pistols are hungry and our tempers are short
So bring your daughters around to the fort
'Cause we're the cops of the world, boys
We're the cops of the world . . .

We own half the world, oh say can you see?
And the name for our profits is democracy
So like it or not, you will have to be free
'Cause we're the cops of the world, boys
We're the cops of the world

At the same time that U.S. imperialism was crowing more loudly, a peace movement was growing around the world and in the United States. There was even an Anti-Imperialist League with voices like Mark Twain's, and quotations from Jefferson, Madison, and Monroe used to argue against imperialism.

In 1905 in the *Atlantic* magazine, Charles F. Dole, whose son would create a pineapple republic in Hawaii, but who was himself Chairman of the Association to Abolish War, published an article arguing that if the Monroe Doctrine had ever served any purpose, that time was passed. Not one European nation had any designs on the Western Hemisphere, and those that had promoted monarchy were by now constitutional republics. International law was now capable of handling financial disputes. The last thing anyone needed was militarism.[102] But the Monroe Doctrine was too valuable to be abandoned. With the excuse of autocratic European threats gone, the doctrine simply had to openly admit to U.S. imperial designs, even while preserving some modified patina of benevolence.

Theodore Roosevelt was involved in both war and peace, if more centrally in the former. He favored the use of arbitration in place of war wherever a war held no interest for him, even while celebrating war as a desirable end in itself. In 1906, he was rather absurdly awarded a Nobel Peace Prize. The Nobel Foundation, which seems not to have included a word of hesitation or misgiving on its webpages about such honorees as Henry Kissinger and Barack Obama, has this to say about its award to Roosevelt:

"Imperialist and Peace Arbitrator

"Theodore Roosevelt, President of the USA, received the Peace Prize for having negotiated peace in the Russo-Japanese war in 1904-5. He also resolved a dispute with Mexico by resorting to arbitration as recommended by the peace movement. Roosevelt was the first statesman to be awarded the Peace Prize, and for the first time the award was controversial. The Norwegian Left argued that Roosevelt

was a 'military mad' imperialist who completed the American conquest of the Philippines. Swedish newspapers wrote that Alfred Nobel was turning in his grave, and that Norway awarded the Peace Prize to Roosevelt in order to win powerful friends after the dramatic dissolution of the union with Sweden the previous year."[103]

Roosevelt Corollary

This is a famous one. In his 1904 State of the Union Address, President Theodore Roosevelt included these words:

"All that this country desires is to see the neighboring countries stable, orderly, and prosperous. Any country whose people conduct themselves well can count upon our hearty friendship. If a nation shows that it knows how to act with reasonable efficiency and decency in social and political matters, if it keeps order and pays its obligations, it need fear no interference from the United States. Chronic wrongdoing, or an impotence which results in a general loosening of the ties of civilized society, may in America, as elsewhere, ultimately require intervention by some civilized nation, and in the Western Hemisphere the adherence of the United States to the Monroe Doctrine may force the United States, however reluctantly, in flagrant cases of such wrongdoing or impotence, to the exercise of an international police power."

While these words claim that the Monroe Doctrine may force a reluctant United States into wars, as if the words of an earlier speech can do that, they have been regularly treated as a new doctrine because they explicitly state things that the Monroe Doctrine did not, and because they were uttered at a time when U.S. imperialism outside of North America was increasing. Within the boundaries of the United States, Roosevelt, in the same very long speech, which touched on many topics, urged a reduction in supplies to "savage" Native Americans deprived of their lands and lifestyles, in order to teach them how to work and become "civilized." He urged that the wrong sorts of people not be admitted as immigrants to the United States. He promoted the settler-colonizing of Alaska, Hawaii, and Puerto Rico. He spoke in support of war as international "policing." He also, perhaps contradictorily, spoke in support of the Hague conferences and of creating treaties of arbitration. And he led into the sentences that became a doctrine with this sentence: "It is not true that the United States feels any land hunger or entertains any projects as regards the other nations of the Western Hemisphere save such as are for their welfare" -- a sentence perhaps even less self-aware than its speaker's claim to carry a "big stick," and certainly less self-aware than the shapers of the Doctrine who have chosen to omit it.

Roosevelt went on to advocate for wars even when no U.S. "interests" could be found, wars for the sake of humanity: "In asserting the Monroe Doctrine, in taking such steps as we have taken in regard to Cuba, Venezuela, and Panama, and in endeavoring to circumscribe the theater of war in the Far East, and to secure the open door in China, we have acted in our own interest as well as in the interest of humanity at large. There are, however, cases in which, while our own interests are not greatly involved, strong appeal is made to our sympathies. . . . The cases in which we could interfere by force of arms as we interfered to put a stop to intolerable conditions in Cuba are necessarily very few. Yet . . . ." Later in the speech, Roosevelt went on to justify occupation of the Philippines, because "they are utterly incapable of existing in independence at all or of building up a civilization of their own."[104]

While the Roosevelt Corollary was spoken, and made into a doctrine, and widely discussed at a time when U.S. imperialism had moved well beyond the continental U.S., it was an amendment to, not a reversal of, the original Monroe Doctrine. As we will see below, the Monroe Doctrine itself included and was quickly used to justify imperialism both within and beyond North America. Roosevelt's explicit references to launching wars are significant, of course, as is his declaration that, in effect, wars should be disguised as humanitarian and philanthropic enterprises. But just as significant may be his abandonment of the limitation of doctrines to the Western Hemisphere, effectively going global with the Monroe-Roosevelt Doctrine of warmaking.

Since 1907, all parties to the Hague Convention of 1907 have been obliged to "use their best efforts to ensure the pacific settlement of international differences," to appeal to other nations to mediate, to accept offers of mediation from other nations, to create if needed "an International Commission of Inquiry, to facilitate a solution of these disputes by elucidating the facts by means of an impartial and conscientious investigation" and to appeal if needed to the permanent court at the Hague for arbitration. Violation of this treaty would later be the second charge in the 1945 Nuremberg Indictment of Nazis. Parties to the convention, which is understood by the United States as replacing that of 1899, have always included the United States and enough nations to effectively eliminate war if it were complied with.

In 1907, the U.S. added a reservation to its ratification of the treaty, similar to what it had added in 1899. Then it came back in 1909 and added that the United States would not submit to arbitration by the permanent court unless it had specifically agreed to do so through a separate treaty with the other party in a dispute. When the World Court would rule against the United States in the 1980s for its crime of mining a harbor in Nicaragua, the United States would simply ignore the ruling. And yet, good global citizen that it is, the U.S. government would bother to add a further reservation to the 1907 convention in 2015 stipulating its belief that Palestine had no right to join the agreement that the United States openly defied.[105] U.S. military actions in the Western Hemisphere in the 1900s included:

1901 Panama
1901-1902 Colombia
1903 Dominican Republic
1903 Honduras
1903-1914 Panama
1904 Dominican Republic
1906-1909 Cuba
1907 Honduras
1909-1910 Nicaragua

U.S. interventions in Central America, Mexico, and Cuba were in the 1910s just normal parts of the scenery, but local coups played as large a role as U.S. military actions, though sometimes the two were combined. Reinforcing the Monroe Doctrine was standard operating procedure. In 1912, a Japanese syndicate tried to acquire a portion of Baja California from Mexico. After the creation of the Lodge Corollary, forbidding such an act under the Monroe Doctrine, the deal was never completed. The Panama Canal finally opened in 1914.

Lodge Corollary

This is nowhere near as famous as Roosevelt's. In 1912 Senator Henry Cabot Lodge proposed and the Senate passed a statement that forbade nations or companies from outside the Western Hemisphere to acquire sufficient territory in the Western Hemisphere to control it.

In 1909 Nicaragua's president was José Santos Zelaya, who was destined to be overthrown, but whose overthrow is not to be confused with the U.S.-backed overthrow 100 years later in 2009 in Honduras of President Manuel Zelaya. The Zelaya in 1909 in Nicaragua displeased U.S. business interests and therefore displeased U.S. President William Howard Taft and Secretary of State Philander Chase Knox, whose law firm represented one of the business interests. As had worked to gin up the war against Spain, wild accusations were made in U.S. newspapers, and by Knox, about Zelaya. The U.S. armed both Nicaraguan rebels and the Nicaraguan government, the former more so to help it win, the latter just for the money. While wars without U.S.-made weapons on both sides are a rarity today, back then weapons dealing was still something that could be criticized. The U.S. also sent in the Marines, under the command of Smedley Butler. First Zelaya fled, and then his successor. But the replacement government didn't work out too well, and in 1912 Smedley Butler and the Marines returned for an occupation that would last until 1933.

Taft declared that, "the day is not far distant when three Stars and Stripes at three equidistant points will mark our territory: one at the North Pole, another at the Panama Canal, and the third at the South Pole. The whole hemisphere will be ours in fact as, by virtue of our superiority of race, it already is ours morally."[106]

I hope you'll indulge me here by considering the story of an individual that I think adds much to our understanding of the early 20th century Monroe Doctrine, although his story -- like the uses of the Monroe Doctrine -- strays beyond the Western Hemisphere.

Smedley Butler is sometimes left out of basic U.S. history lessons. He is most famous for having prevented a Wall Street coup against Franklin Roosevelt. Also a scandal erupted when he recounted how Mussolini had run over a little girl with his car. But Butler's most famous piece of writing is called "War Is a Racket." In it, he said things like this: "War is a racket. It always has been. It is possibly the oldest, easily the most profitable, surely the most vicious. It is the only one international in scope. It is the only one in which the profits are reckoned in dollars and the losses in lives."

Butler also spent years denouncing the slow and steady buildup toward World War II, the arms race and provocations of Japan, the anti-Japanese propaganda driven by U.S. financial interests in China, the support for Nazis and Fascists in Europe. Why, he demanded to know, for at least five years until his death in 1940, did the U.S. Navy not hold its war rehearsals near California instead of near Japan?

But Smedley is not left out of peace activist history. If you've ever done a bit of peace activism in the United States, you likely know all about Smedley Butler, or think you do. I thought I did. As an advisory board member of Veterans For Peace, one chapter of which is named for Smedley, and having read numerous account's of Smedley's exploits including David

Talbot's *Devil Dog*, having seen reenactors dress up as Smedley and recite some of his famous words, having dug up old Smedley speeches such as the one he gave here in Charlottesville, I figured I knew a bit about the guy. Then I read Jonathan Katz's book, *Gangsters of Capitalism*.[107]

Butler famously said: "I spent thirty- three years and four months in active military service as a member of this country's most agile military force, the Marine Corps. I served in all commissioned ranks from Second Lieutenant to Major-General. And during that period, I spent most of my time being a high class muscle- man for Big Business, for Wall Street and for the Bankers. In short, I was a racketeer, a gangster for capitalism."

The thing is, Smedley meant it. He'd spent decades roving the world for the U.S. government, overthrowing democracies, propping up dictators, slaughtering and enslaving the local people. If there were any statues of Smedley in our city squares, they could get pulled down for racism. If we ever started pulling down statues for senseless mass killing, they could get pulled down for that.

Smedley Butler claimed that the war racket profited the rich while punishing primarily the U.S. soldiers. And he did live right up through the moment in which big wars shifted from killing mainly soldiers to killing mainly civilians. But Smedley's wars of Central American, Caribbean, and Asian empire killed mainly the devalued inhabitants of the places where they were waged, and inflicted major damage on entire populations that could last for a century or more.

Whistleblowers are an odd lot. We think of Smedley as having been innocent of the Business Plot coup and having blown the whistle on other people. And then we think of him as having blown the whistle on the Marine Corps and the U.S. military. But do we stop and understand that the military evil he denounced he was not only a part of but was often in charge of — or at least pretty high up in the ranks? Do we stop to note that he volunteered — eagerly, and repeatedly?

We brag that Smedley was the most decorated U.S. Marine, because how cool is that for the antiwar veteran to have more medals than the corrupt war pigs? But why did he have those medals? Why did he have two — count em, two — Medals of Honor? One was for attacking the inhabitants of Veracruz, Mexico, in an action so atrocious that a record number of medals were handed out to make defeating civilians, including untrained women and boys fighting back against foreign invasion, seem glorious. The other was for chasing Haitians intent on independence and guilty of wanting-freedom-while-black to the last possible fort at the top of the last possible mountain and then killing them.

Yes, Smedley defied orders from bureaucrats in order to look out for his rank and file troops. Yes, Smedley supported the Bonus Army of impoverished veterans camped out in Washington D.C. where they were attacked by MacArthur and Eisenhower (after Smedley had left). Yes, Smedley was courageous beyond all measure. Yes, Smedley was a Northern Quaker (I think you'd have to say non-practicing) with less racism than many Southerners. Yes, he gradually tired of war and sought to prevent pointless conflicts during his last gig in China. But Smedley's career had a jumpstart and a steady boost from the fact that his father was in Congress on the House Committee on Naval Affairs. And Smedley is famous for confessing to atrocities, to horrors beyond any possible moral defense. And Smedley was as slow as any whistleblower to wake up to what he was engaged in. Smedley was old and already retired when he finally came around. If you watch the Snowden movie and scream at the screen over how long it takes him to snap out of it, just notice what a young man he still is at the end. Dan Ellsberg's long career as a peace activist began after his whistleblowing.

To write *Gangsters of Capitalism*, Katz traveled the world to the places Smedley had been. He found Haitians recalling him as a brutal foreign despot who had forced men to work on roads unpaid on pain of death. He found populations around the world with museums and reenactments of outrages that the people of the United States, which inflicted them, have little memory of — a fact that is incomprehensible to some of the victims of U.S. imperialism.

Smedley Butler began with the betrayal of Cuba, followed by the brutal killing and torture in the Philippines, seeking out neither U.S. empire nor a delusion of benevolent paternalism so much as the manhood of participation in violence no matter its purpose. His next victims were Chinese. Katz quotes a U.S. general estimating that civilians to Chinese fighters killed were in a proportion of about 50 to 1. Some 100,000 Chinese were killed. Katz finds people in the Philippines still angry, and the people of China intent on undoing long-ago but not forgotten humiliations — humiliations not of them but of their nation. Butler, years later, regretted looting Beijing. I don't know if he regretted killing people there — but it seems that in general and in some cases in particular eventually he did regret all the killing, even if he mostly regretted the deaths of U.S. Marines.

Butler helped steal the land for and build the Panama Canal and bring the U.S. racist apartheid system to the canal zone, where the residents were forcibly displaced, mostly black workers often died on the job, and the Marines served as the thugs of the bosses. He helped stamp out self-governance in Nicaragua, inspiring the resistance of Augusto Sandino who would in turn inspire the Sandinistas. He committed his horrors in Mexico and Haiti. He effectively ruled Haiti, as Walker had Nicaragua, but with the full support of the U.S. government.

Butler developed "counter-insurgency" practices before they were called that. Rather than bringing freedom of religion — or even anything Quaker

— to Haiti, Butler went after the Vodou religion, arresting priests and burning shrines. Butler helped install the dictatorship of Trujillo in the Dominican Republic. He took over the Haitian parliament at gunpoint and threatened to slaughter the lot of them, while the U.S. was famously jumping into World War I to keep the world safe for "democracy." A Haitian novel concludes with the slow and painful killing of a Butler character named "Smedley Seaton."

Butler developed military police forces, sometimes known as death squads, in Central America. He helped militarize U.S. police departments, personally running the Philadelphia police, during which time he trained, among others, the future notoriously racist police chief and mayor Frank Rizzo. Before Butler went after the prohibition-violating kingpins and got himself fired, his alcohol war disproportionately targeted African-Americans. And he instructed his troops to kill.

Butler helped Hollywood generate pro-Marines propaganda, including Lon Chaney's top-grossing hit, *Tell It To the Marines*. Who can weigh the impact of that against Butler's later antiwar speeches?

Butler was involved in countless shadow wars that have been erased from U.S. history, some of which led to dictatorships still alive and well, others of which led to massive blowback, one of which led eventually to the revolution in China. Butler was sent to China the last time by Frank Kellogg, who had recently been maneuvered by peace activists into backing a treaty banning war. The United States was becoming an imperial force for which sending troops somewhere wasn't necessarily a war. It might be a police action.

When Butler took a break and tried running a coal mine in West Virginia, his vicious, violent Marine approach resulted in the workers trying to kill him. He decided he'd be safer in the Marine Corps and went right back to it. But eventually — as often happens, it was post-retirement — he had a change in his thinking. And he came out swinging and named names.

> *"I helped make Mexico, especially Tampico, safe for American oil interests in 1914," Butler later said. "I helped make Haiti and Cuba a decent place for the National City Bank boys to collect revenues in. I helped in the raping of half a dozen Central American republics for the benefits of Wall Street. The record of racketeering is long. I helped purify Nicaragua for the international banking house of Brown Brothers in 1909-1912. I brought light to the Dominican Republic for American sugar interests in 1916. In China I helped to see to it that Standard Oil went its way unmolested."*

How did Smedley change his mind? Katz does a good job of finding hints and subtle shifts through the years, and notes that when Butler started recounting tales of anti-democratic thuggery abroad he was at first shocked that the U.S. public was shocked, that people were blissfully unaware of what their government routinely did. The realization that nobody knew — and that those who did preferred not to talk about it — may have helped motivate Butler to tell. Yet when he told on Wall Street coup plotters, his qualifications for reporting that plot to a Congressional Committee were not usually explained in terms of his expertise in recognizing coups by virtue of having participated in more of them than possibly anyone else alive. That point never quite came through to general understanding.

The fact that a bunch of U.S. imperial bases, deeply resented by the local inhabitants, and named for Smedley Butler, today take up a great deal of land in Okinawa, is an insult to who Butler became, but an acknowledgement of who he had been for a much longer part of his life.

Not just Roosevelt's Corollary, but also Smedley Butler's career, can be found germinating in the language of the original Monroe Doctrine, which assumed power over other nations. But none of it was necessary. Other paths could have been chosen at any point, and still could.

The major development in the 1910s for war and peace was the Great War (World War I) which saw peace movements crushed and dissolved. It also effectively put an end to the idea of the United States staying out of European wars, and did so through the development of the modern propaganda campaign.

U.S. military actions in the Western Hemisphere in the 1910s included:

1911-1912 Honduras
1912 Cuba
1912-1933 Nicaragua
1914 Dominican Republic
1914 Haiti
1914-1919 Mexico
1915-1934 Haiti
1916-1924 Dominican Republic
1917-1922 Cuba
1918-1921 Panama
1919-1920 Honduras

In the 1920s peace was in the air or at least on the mind. World War I had been fought as a war to end war, and both those who believed the propaganda and those who did not wanted that to be true. Probably the biggest, most widespread and mainstream peace movement and war abolition movement the United States has seen was seen in the 1920s and into the 1930s.

In 1917, President Woodrow Wilson, in the same speech in which he had advocated for a peace without victory, had claimed that the Monroe Doctrine meant the freedom of every country to be left free and independent. Wilson had proposed that the whole world adopt that Monroe Doctrine:

> *"I am proposing, as it were, that the nations should with one accord adopt the doctrine of President Monroe as the doctrine of the world: that no nation should seek to extend its polity over any other nation or people, but that every people should be left free to determine its own polity, its own way of development--unhindered, unthreatened, unafraid, the little along with the great and powerful."*

Wilson said this while continuing and even escalating the military and financial campaigns of his predecessors to control Mexico and Central America. And, of course, the peace made after the war was a peace of vindictive punishment, predicted by wise observers on the spot to create a sequel within 20 years.[108]

In an excellent column on the history of the Monroe Doctrine published in 1984 in the *New York Times* Yale professor Gaddis Smith wrote:

> *"President Woodrow Wilson expanded American intervention under the Monroe Doctrine. He did emphasize an American mission to nurture democratic ideals rather than the necessity of protecting American security, but the results for the countries being controlled were the same no matter what the rhetorical justification."*[109]

Wilson also wanted the United States to join the League of Nations and ran up against the Monroe Doctrine as an argument against it. He actually got a Monroe Doctrine exception written into the text of the Covenant creating the League of Nations: "Nothing in this Covenant shall be deemed to affect the validity of international engagements, such as treaties of arbitration or regional understandings like the Monroe Doctrine, for securing the maintenance of peace." But even that failed to win over the U.S. Senate, which had very little interest in being one nation among equals. After all, the Monroe Doctrine was not an "international engagement" or "regional understanding." It was just some stuff a U.S. president had said.

The Senate Foreign Relations Committee proposed at one point joining the League of Nations but stipulating that the Monroe Doctrine would be wholly outside of it and interpreted solely by the United States.

Between the presidencies of Woodrow Wilson and Franklin Roosevelt was a period of three presidencies of extremely little interest to U.S. history texts, because global mass slaughter had eased up for a sort of extended half-time show between the two world wars. From 1921 to 1933, Warren G. Harding, Calvin Coolidge, and Herbert Hoover continued U.S. imperialism south of the border and elsewhere on the planet, but with nothing remotely on the scale of the world wars, and with various steps even taken in the direction of peace, albeit while continuing to invest in weaponry and plan for wars and to cite the Monroe Doctrine as an exception to any peace plan.

In 1923, the Monroe Doctrine turned 100 and was celebrated with a half-dollar coin. Some 10 million school children listened to the Doctrine being read and discussed, just as if it were the Declaration of Independence on the Fourth of July. It was read on the radio. It was discussed in the newspapers. Mary Baker Eddy, founder of the Christian Science religion said, "I believe strictly in the Monroe Doctrine, in our Constitution and in the laws of God."

The story of peace activism in this period, and of the successful creation in 1928 of the Kellogg-Briand Pact, is one that I've tried to tell in my book *When the World Outlawed War*. Since 1928, all parties to the Kellogg-Briand Pact have been legally required to "condemn recourse to war for the solution of international controversies, and renounce it, as an instrument of national policy in their relations with one another," and to "agree that the settlement or solution of all disputes or conflicts of whatever nature or of whatever origin they may be, which may arise among them, shall never be sought except by pacific means." Violation of this treaty would go on to become Charge XIII in the 1945 Nuremberg Indictment of Nazis. Parties to the Pact have always included enough nations to effectively eliminate war by complying with it.

In fact, most nations on Earth either joined the Pact or were joined by their hypocritical colonizers. The glaring exceptions were Mexico, El Salvador, Colombia, Ecuador, Brazil, Bolivia, Paraguay, Uruguay, and Argentina — in other words, much of the area targeted by the Monroe Doctrine. Mongolia, Nepal, San Marino, Yemen, and what is now Saudi Arabia were the only other exceptions. The nations of Latin America had learned to distrust U.S. commitments.

While the U.S. government ratified the Kellogg-Briand Pact without adding a formal reservation stipulating that it didn't really mean it -- having been under tremendous public pressure not to pull any such stunt, the Senate Foreign Relations Committee nonetheless published a report "interpreting" the treaty to allow the Monroe Doctrine.

During the many months of campaigning to create the Kellogg-Briand Pact, the British House of Lords passed a resolution backing the U.S. proposal "whilst recognizing the desire of His Majesty's Government to cooperate in securing the peace of the world." There was little doubt that "securing peace" meant waging war. On May 19, 1928, Britain sent the United States a note that expressed concern over British imperial interests, paralleling U.S. concern over the Monroe Doctrine. A statement by Secretary of State for Foreign Affairs Austen Chamberlain came to be known in the press as the "British Monroe Doctrine."

U.S. Senator John Blaine remarked in the Senate in 1928: "We have turned the Monroe Doctrine into an agency of mischief for America, not for her protection or the protection of weaker nations and peoples (but as an instrument that made American intervention), the wet nurse for alien governments, money lenders, adventurers, and concession-grabbers in their career of expansion, extension, and exploitation."

The U.S. Senate did approve joining the World Court at the Hague, but added a reservation claiming absolute freedom of action under the Monroe Doctrine.

In 1928, but not made public until 1930, U.S. Undersecretary of State J. Reuben Clark wrote the Clark Memorandum -- not something that anyone has elevated to the list of doctrines, but still a statement understood to impact the Monroe Doctrine, although from reading it, it is not clear how. The thing reads like a high school essay on the hundredth anniversary of the Doctrine, summarizing what it is and what it does. But the general interpretation was and is that this memorandum partially repudiated the Roosevelt Corollary -- an interpretation likely based on the tone of the memo and on contemporary actions.[110]

While all this discussion of peace plans was underway, the U.S. government and U.S. corporations were devouring Central America. United Fruit and other U.S. companies had acquired their own land, their own railways, their own mail and telegraph and telephone services, and their own politicians. Noted Eduardo Galeano: "in Honduras, a mule costs more than a deputy, and throughout Central America U.S. ambassadors do more presiding than presidents." The United Fruit Company created its own ports, its own customs, and its own police. The dollar became the local currency. When a strike broke out in Colombia, police slaughtered banana workers, just as government thugs would do for U.S. companies in Colombia for many decades to come.[111]

But partisan divides were creating debates in Washington D.C. where Congress Members were introducing resolutions to remove U.S. troops from Nicaragua. Senator Burton Wheeler in 1927 said, "The State Department has literally gutted the sovereignty of Nicaragua. At this moment it has the little republic hog-tied. . . . Every strategic post, fiscal and military, is in the hands of the appointees of the State Department." Of course, this was true, so President Coolidge needed to counter it with a lie. He chose to claim that Mexico was planning to take over Nicaragua and . . . wait for it . . . wait for it . . . turn Nicaragua communist. This claim had no more basis in the 1920s than in the 1980s or at any other point in the illustrious history of the Monroe Doctrine. Secretary Kellogg -- he of the treaty banning war -- presented the Senate Foreign Relations Committee with a statement on "Bolshevist Aims and Policies in Latin America" that included no evidence of anything. It also didn't work. Just as Lyndon Johnson would do in 1965 for his war on the Dominican Republic, Coolidge abandoned the communist plot rationale that nobody was swallowing and shifted to a claim of needing to protect U.S. lives in Nicaragua, plus a Monroe Doctrine claim to be protecting the place from the British.

In Nicaragua, the U.S.-backed dictator, who wanted the U.S. to annex Nicaragua (but the U.S. public and government did not want that) was losing battles to a rebel named Augusto César Sandino. The U.S. Marine Corps fared no better against Sandino. Sandino drafted a "Plan for the Realization of the Great Dream of Bolivar," which included the abolition of the Monroe Doctrine. After years of fighting, in 1933 the United States would withdraw the Marines in defeat. But in 1934, Sandino would be assassinated by the head of the army Anastasio Somoza, who would state that U.S. Ambassador Arthur Bliss Lane had ordered the execution. Somoza would go on to rule over a bloody terrorizing government for a quarter century, and establish a family dynasty.

U.S. military actions in the Western Hemisphere in the 1920s, 1930s, and 1940s included:

1925 Panama
1932 El Salvador

By the time Hoover was president, if not before, the U.S. government had generally caught on that people in Latin America understood the words "Monroe Doctrine" to mean Yankee imperialism. Hoover announced that the Monroe Doctrine did not justify military interventions. Hoover and then Franklin Roosevelt withdrew U.S. troops from Central America until they remained only in the Canal Zone. FDR said he would have a "good neighbor" policy.

Hoover-Stimson or Stimson Doctrine

This doctrine is usually not included, perhaps because it runs counter to all the others. Following the banning of all war by the 1928 Kellogg-Briand Pact[112], in 1932 Secretary of State under President Herbert Hoover, Henry Stimson, articulated the doctrine of non-recognition of territorial gains made through war. When Russia invaded China in 1929, world governments successfully pressured Russia to withdraw in compliance with the Kellogg-Briand Pact. When Japan invaded China in 1931, Stimson articulated his doctrine, which had been stated similarly in 1919 by Salmon Levinson, key advocate for the creation of the Kellogg-Briand Pact. The League of Nations also told Japan its gains would not be recognized. And they were not, and the Stimson doctrine is effectively international law today, but of course Japan did not leave China until the worst war yet waged had come and gone and Stimson had put in five more years in his second stint as Secretary of War.

Another reason for speaking less of the Monroe Doctrine in the United States was how Japan and Germany began speaking of it, criticizing U.S. imperialism in Latin America. Both Japan and Germany had learned something about public relations from the United States. Japan had also learned something about imperialism from the U.S. FDR not only built up an array of U.S. bases in the Pacific, but also traded old ships to England in exchange for the lease of its bases in the Caribbean and Bermuda.

The Good Neighbor policy included speaking differently about and to Latin American governments, including meeting with them. FDR attended a Pan-American Union meeting in Buenos Aires in 1936. Secretary of State Cordell Hull attended a Pan-American Conference in Lima in 1938, which produced a joint declaration by 21 nations committed vaguely to collective opposition to any foreign intervention.[113] The Good Neighbor policy also included annulling the Platt Amendment in 1934.

The Good Neighbor policy did not include repairing much of the damage that previous policies had contributed to. Years of U.S. interventions had helped create brutal dictatorships in Nicaragua, Haiti, Cuba, and the Dominican Republic, and now they were respectfully left to their own devices (and a new coup government in El Salvador in 1936 was respectfully recognized by the United States). The people in these countries had a hard time believing the U.S. was really staying out of their affairs, and by the time they believed it, it would no longer be true -- if it ever was. While staying out of Nicaraguan elections, FDR nonetheless welcomed the Nicaraguan dictator to Washington and reportedly and famously remarked, "He's a sonofabitch but he's our sonofabitch."

In 1939 Warner Brothers released a 16-minute film about the Monroe Doctrine that invented dialog in a cabinet meeting with President James Monroe, in which Monroe supposedly foresaw that he was creating a permanent Doctrine for the defense of "democracy" against anti-democratic foreign dictators, and John Quincy Adams supposedly gave it the name "Monroe Doctrine " the moment the speech was drafted. [114] The most noble character trait, this film suggests, is a willingness to wage war. The film provides a selective and fictionalized history of the uses of the Monroe Doctrine. First, we marvel at President Polk's defense of California through which he "makes it plain that the people of the American continents alone have the right to decide their own destiny" -- an odd description of a war of conquest. Then we see President Millard Fillmore in 1852 supposedly extending the meaning of the Doctrine by threatening war with England and France over Cuba. Of course, Fillmore was busy supporting U.S.

filibusterers in Cuba. Next, the U.S. in 1866 supposedly safeguard's Mexico by threatening war on France. And in 1895 President Grover Cleveland is shown threatening war to protect Venezuela from an unnamed "foreign power." (Was England not named because it was not true that Cleveland had threatened war, or because of what was happening in Europe in 1939?) Theodore Roosevelt makes it into the movie, but only in 1905 for supposedly rescuing Santo Domingo (the Dominican Republic) from imperialism by being willing to threaten war in the name of peace. Roosevelt is given the final word in this propaganda film to deliver a mishmash of the sorts of things Roosevelt actually said about war being a great opportunity for honor and yet serving only the purpose of maintaining peace.

Peace was still in the air into the 1930s. The U.S. Congress held public hearings on the shame of weapons dealers profiting from World War I. But the biggest war was brewing, and it would impact every bit of the world, even Latin America. [115] Far from keeping Europe out of Latin America and itself out of European wars, the United States would help drag Latin America into a European war.

Mexican oil fueled Nazi Germany. Brazil's forests were sacrificed for failed U.S. attempts to produce rubber using, among other outrages, forced child labor. Jewish refugees from Europe were shamefully turned away from Latin America — with various small exceptions. People of German and Japanese ancestry were hauled from some countries north to the United States to prison camps, or to forced labor in Panama. The United States built military bases in Central America, and sent lend-lease weaponry meant to oppose Germany to, instead, prop op Latin American dictators.

During WWII, the U.S. used Central American resources, such as rubber and citronella, to replace those under Japanese control, as well as mahogany for building PT boats. By mid-1943, 95 percent of exports from Nicaragua were to the United States.[116] The U.S. used the Export-Import bank and the

Inter-American Development Commission to compel nations to engage in free trade with the U.S., use no tariffs to protect local industries, and effectively limit their economies to products not produced in the United States. Upon the end of the war, the U.S. would create the International Monetary Fund (IMF) and the World Bank which would serve much the same purpose for many years to come.

The United States, for war propaganda purposes, sought to build friendly relations between the U.S. and Latin American peoples, in particular in Brazil. There were limitations, as Nelson Rockefeller apparently did not want Orson Welles filming poor or black people.

The two sides of World War II spied on each other in Latin America, sank each other's ships off the coast, and left their traces behind. Brazilians fought with the Allies in Italy, and veterans of that fighting established a U.S.-backed military dictatorship in Brazil from 1964 to 1985 — a tradition Brazil has not yet completely left behind.

Argentina set up its own form of fascism under Juan Perón, and rat lines (systems of escape routes) to Argentina became the Catholic Church's retirement plan for Nazis not tried at Nuremberg and not included in Operation Paperclip — rat lines also used by Allen Dulles and U.S. "intelligence" types to protect Nazis. While Costa Rica abolished its military in 1948 and has benefited ever since, most of Latin America became more heavily militarized, including with U.S. bases.

Latin America was also instrumental in getting the United States into World War II in the first place. FDR claimed to have a Nazi map depicting Nazi plans for conquering and re-organizing South America. Ivar Bryce -- Walter Lippman's brother-in-law, Ian Fleming's buddy, and an employee of James Bond-model William Stephenson in a British operation to get the United States into the war -- claimed in a memoir to have produced the first draft of the map.[117] So this appears to have been a British or British-American operation to get the United States to defend Latin America by joining a European war, an odd twist on the Monroe Doctrine. This was FDR's warning in October 1941:

> *"I have in my possession a secret map made in Germany by Hitler's government-by the planners of the new world order. It is a map of South America and a part of Central America, as Hitler proposes to reorganize it. Today in this area there are fourteen separate countries. The geographical experts of Berlin, however, have ruthlessly obliterated all existing boundary lines; and have divided South America into five vassal states, bringing the whole continent under their domination. And they have also so arranged it that the territory of one of these new puppet states includes the Republic of Panama and our great life line-the Panama Canal. That is his plan. It will never go into effect. This map makes clear the Nazi design not only against South America but against the United States itself."*

FDR edited this speech to remove an assertion as to the map's authenticity. He refused to show the map to the media or the public. He did not say where the map came from, how he connected it to Hitler, or how it depicted a design against the United States, or — for that matter — how one might have sliced up Latin America and not included Panama. *Life* magazine push-polled readers on whether they supported defending all of the Americas from Germany. A strong majority did.[118]

By the end of World War II, the United States was viewing synthetics as an alternative to many tropical raw materials, and the airplane as an alternative to many colonial outposts. The United States actually freed the Philippines from overt colonization.

In 1948, the ninth International Conference of American States was held in Bogotá at which U.S. Secretary of State George Marshall had members pledge to fight against communism in the Western Hemisphere. Out of this meeting came the modern Organization of American States (OAS) headquartered in Washington, D.C.

Truman Doctrine

On March 12, 1947, in a lengthy speech to Congress, President Harry Truman said, "I believe it must be the policy of the United States to support free peoples who are resisting attempted subjugation by armed minorities or by outside pressures. I believe that we must assist free peoples to work out their own destinies in their own way. I believe that our help should be primarily through economic and financial aid which is essential to economic stability and orderly political processes."[119] By "free" Truman was widely understood to mean non-Soviet. He was seeking aid for a Greek monarchy. Nonetheless, the Truman Doctrine lies in the tradition of the Monroe Doctrine's division of the world into democratic and monarchical governments, and President Joe Biden's division of the world into the Rules Based Order and everyone else. For decades, aiding governments that aligned with the United States against the Soviet Union, as well as sabotaging governments that aligned with the Soviet Union or were even vaguely suspected of considering doing so, was standard operating procedure. So was waging wars on this same justification, even if Truman had said that "primarily" the United States should provide aid. In the same speech Truman promoted the idea of falling dominoes that would be used to scare people into supporting wars in Korea, Vietnam, and elsewhere. In other speeches that seem to have collectively contributed to the concept of the Truman Doctrine, Truman spoke of Soviet communism as a disease that needed to be contained, just as the Holy Alliance had needed to be contained in Monroe's day.

By the 1950s the United States was not claiming to be a good neighbor so much as the boss of the protection-against-communism service. This was the era of the Kennan Corollary and the Eisenhower Doctrine, an age of U.S.-instigated coups. After successfully creating a coup in Iran in 1953, the U.S. turned to Latin America. At the tenth Pan-America Conference in Caracas in 1954, Secretary of State John Foster Dulles supported the Monroe Doctrine and claimed that Soviet communism was a threat to Guatemala.

Kennan Corollary

In 1950, U.S. diplomat George F. Kennan declared that communism must be kept out of Latin America, even if oppressive tactics were required: "We cannot be too dogmatic about the methods by which local Communists can be dealt with. . . . Where the concepts and traditions of popular government are too weak to absorb successfully the intensity of Communist attack, then we must concede that harsh governmental measures of repression may be the only answer; that these measures may have to proceed from regimes whose origins and methods would not stand the test of American concepts of democratic procedure; and that such regimes and such methods may be preferable alternatives, and indeed the only alternatives, to further Communist successes."[120]

Edward Bernays had been hired in 1944 by United Fruit. A veteran of the Committee on Public Information which had marketed World War I, nephew of Sigmund Freud, and father of the noble profession of exploiting and encouraging human irrationality through "public relations," Bernays, had published a book in 1928 called sim-ply *Propaganda*, which actually propagandized for the merits of propaganda. Bernays helped United Fruit's Sam Zemurray (who had overthrown the president of Honduras in 1911) by creating a PR campaign beginning in 1951 in the United States against the overly democratic government of Guatemala. The *New York Times* and other media outlets followed Bernays's lead, depicting the noble United Fruit as suffering under the rule of a Marxist dictatorship—which was actually an elected government implementing New Deal- type reforms.

Senator Henry Cabot Lodge Jr. (R-MA) led the effort in Congress. He was the great-great-great-grandson of Senator George Cabot (F-MA) and grandson of Senator Henry Cabot Lodge (R-MA) who had pushed the country into the Spanish-American War and World War I, defeated the League of Nations, and built up the Navy. Henry Cabot Lodge Jr. would go on to serve as ambassador to South Vietnam, a position in which he would help maneuver the nation into the Vietnam War. While the Soviet Union had no relations with Guatemala, the father of the CIA Allen Dulles was certain or claimed to be certain that Moscow was directing Guatemala's fictional march toward communism. With President Dwight Eisenhower's approval, the CIA overthrew Guatemala's government on behalf of United Fruit. Key to the operation was the work of Howard Hunt, who would later break into the Watergate for President Richard Nixon, and later still—on his death bed—confess to a role in the assassination of President John F. Kennedy.

Both Dulles brothers worked for United Fruit, and Allen was on its Board; Henry Cabot Lodge Jr. owned lots of United Fruit stock; Eisenhower's secretary Ann Whitman was married to United Fruit public relations man Ed Whitman.

> *"The Fruit Company, Inc. reserved for itself the most succulent piece, the central coast of my own land, the delicate waist of America. It rechristened its territories 'Banana Republics', and over the sleeping dead, over the restless heroes who brought about the greatness, the liberty, and the flags, it established the comic opera: it abolished free will, gave out imperial crowns, encouraged envy, attracted the dictatorship of flies ... flies sticky with submissive blood and marmalade, drunken flies that buzz over the tombs of the people, circus flies, wise flies expert at tyranny." -- Pablo Neruda, "La United Fruit Co." (1950)*

John Foster Dulles proclaimed a victory for the Monroe Doctrine in Guatemala. But it was a victory for brutal dictatorships that would follow for decades. It was a victory for coup plotters and dictatorship supporters in Washington, D.C., who would expand their plans. It was a victory for blowback across Latin America, where the U.S. government was recognized as an enemy. After the CIA later murdered Guevara, cut off his hands, and mailed them to Fidel Castro, his hands were brought out to inspire anti-U.S. fighters.

Meanwhile the United States tried not to even notice that independence advocates from Puerto Rico shot at and nearly assassinated President Truman in 1950, and in 1954 shot 30 bullets in the U.S. Congress, hitting five Congress Members. The U.S. simply couldn't have angry colonies, since it could not have any colonies.

Eisenhower Doctrine

In a January 5, 1957, speech to Congress, President Dwight Eisenhower said of a proposal he was making to protect the Middle East and its oil from Russian communism, "It would, first of all, authorize the United States to cooperate with and assist any nation or group of nations in the general area of the Middle East in the development of economic strength dedicated to the maintenance of national independence. It would, in the second place, authorize the Executive to undertake in the same region programs of military assistance and cooperation with any nation or group of nations which desires such aid. It would, in the third place, authorize such assistance and cooperation to include the employment of the armed forces of the United States to secure and protect the territorial integrity and political independence of such nations, requesting such aid, against overt armed aggression from any nation controlled by International Communism."[121]

This was an exception as doctrines go, in that Eisenhower actually asked Congress to approve it, which Congress did, passing the Middle East Resolution of 1957.[122] Of course it was not a request to declare a particular war, but a Monroe-Doctrine-like request to authorize a whole pile of future wars, similar to the "Authorizations for the Use of Military Force" that were used to launch the wars on Afghanistan and Iraq by President George W. Bush, and then dozens of smaller wars as well.[123] A request to declare a particular war has hardly been seen since 1941, an exception being President Obama's unsuccessful attempt to gain Congressional authorization in 2013 for a war on Syria, which he followed up with a war on Libya despite Congress's opposition. Of course, Eisenhower's defense of the Middle East from Russia, as that of subsequent presidents, was in practice often a defense of the Middle East from Middle Easterners. Eisenhower kicked off a string of new coups with his successful overthrows of governments in Iran (1953) and Guatemala (1954), as well as unsuccessful attempts in Costa Rica, Syria, Indonesia, and Egypt, and plotting the murder of Patrice Lumumba in the Congo that would not happen until Eisenhower was out of office.

U.S.-backed coup attempts in the 1950s included:

Success in Guatemala 1954
Failure in Costa Rica mid-1950s

By the 1960s the Monroe Doctrine was firmly established as a U.S. commitment to keep the Soviets and anything resembling communism out of Latin America. This of course overlapped the longstanding commitment to protect the "interests" of U.S. companies in Latin America. The self-defeating failure of this commitment in Cuba only heightened the determination of the U.S. government to uphold the Monroe Doctrine.

The U.S. had backed the dictatorship defeated in 1959 by the Cuban revolution. When Cuba nationalized U.S. property in 1960, the U.S. launched the economic blockade that has yet to be lifted (though every nation on Earth but the U.S. and Israel have voted at the U.N. to lift it annually for many years). Cuba then turned to the Soviet Union for support, which was forthcoming, especially after the U.S. tried to invade Cuba in the 1961 Bay of Pigs campaign, and to exclude Cuba from the OAS.

On April 19, 1961, the *New York Times* gave its readers a history of the Monroe Doctrine to that point, as an argument for military madness directed toward Cuba:[124]

> *"The United States Government's determination to halt Communist subversion in Latin America, and Cuba in particular, has its roots in the Monroe Doctrine, first outlined 138 years ago. President James Monroe announced in 1823 that the United States would consider any attempt by European powers to extend their 'system' to this hemisphere 'as dangerous to our peace and safety.' The President's unilateral statement gained increasing acceptance as the United States grew stronger, and in the last century has served as a basic precept in this country's hemispheric policies. In the Eighteen Twenties, as now, both Cuba and Russia figured in the formation of the United States' policy toward Latin America. At the time President Monroe made his 'hands off' declaration to the Old World, in his annual message to Congress, it was rumored that Cuba, then a Spanish colony, might be ceded to France. There were also growing fears that Russia might attempt to colonize the Pacific Northwest. The first major challenges to the doctrine came during the Civil War, when Spain annexed the Dominican Republic and French troops occupied Mexico City. Dominican revolutionaries overthrew Spanish rule within a few years and Napoleon III withdrew from Mexico shortly after the war ended as a result of American pressure."*

We've seen how dubious that claim was. The *New York Times* continued:

> *"Monroe's policy came to be considered a permanent 'doctrine' at the turn of the century. Secretary of State Richard Olney referred to it in 1895 when he declared that the United States was 'practically sovereign on this continent.' In that same year, a rebel Cuban junta, directed by Thomas Estrada Palma, an exile in New York, received*

United States sympathy in its efforts to incite a revolt against the Spanish in Cuba. In 1898, the doctrine was invoked as one of the justifications for the Spanish-American war and United States occupation of Cuba, following the blowing up of the battleship Maine in Havana Harbor. The occupation lasted until 1902, when the Republic of Cuba was formed. In 1904, President Theodore Roosevelt added what was known as the 'Roosevelt Corollary' to the Monroe Doctrine. He proclaimed that the United States would act as a 'police power' to force Latin-American republics to honor their obligations to foreign-principally United States-investors. In the years that followed, United States Marines intervened in Dominican Republic, Nicaragua, Cuba and Haiti. In 1933, President Franklin D. Roosevelt repudiated the practice of intervention and instituted a 'Good Neighbor' policy of mutual cooperation.

"Shortly before the United States' entry into World War II, the doctrine was revived as a warning against possible German seizure of the French Islands of Martinique and Guadaloupe after the fall of France in 1940. With the advent of the 'cold war,' the United States took the initiative in attempting to curb the threat of communist subversion. At the Rio conference in 1947, the American republics signed a pact agreeing to consult immediately should any neighboring state 'be affected by an aggression which is not an armed attack.' More importantly, the pact bound the republics in the hemisphere to consider 'an armed attack by any state against an American state as an attack against all the American states.' The republics also vowed to 'assist in meeting' any such attack. When Premier Fidel Castro showed increasing evidence of serving Communist ends, the United States tried, but failed, to expand on the principles of the Rio pact and get other American republics to agree on joint measures to apply sanctions against Cuba. On July 12, 1960, Premier Khrushchev pronounced the Monroe Doctrine dead. Its remains, he said, 'should

best be buried as every dead body is so that it does not poison the air by its decay.'

"President Eisenhower responded by saying that he would 'not permit the establishment of a regime dominated by international communism in the Western Hemisphere.' The State Department followed up the President's statement by reaffirming that 'the principles of the Monroe Doctrine are as valid today as they were in 1823 when the doctrine was proclaimed.' President Kennedy has also applied the doctrine to the Cuban crisis. On April 3 he declared that Dr. Castro's Cuba offered 'a clear and present danger to all the republics of the hemisphere.' He went to call upon Cuba to cast off its Communist ties. 'If this call is unheeded, we are confident that the Cuban people will join hands with other republics in the hemisphere in the struggle to win freedom,' he declared."

On August 29, 1962, President John F. Kennedy was asked about the Monroe Doctrine and replied:[125]

"The Monroe Doctrine means what it has meant since President Monroe and John Quincy Adams enunciated it, and that is that we would oppose a foreign power extending its power to the Western Hemisphere, and that is why we oppose what is happening in Cuba today. That is why we have cut off our trade. That is why we worked in the OAS and in other ways to isolate the Communist menace in Cuba. That is why we will continue to give a good deal of our effort and attention to it."

During the missile crisis that nearly destroyed the world, Kennedy would declare:[126]

"It shall be the policy of this Nation to regard any nuclear missile

> *launched from Cuba against any nation in the Western Hemisphere as an attack by the Soviet Union on the United States, requiring a full retaliatory response upon the Soviet Union."*

Kennedy secretly resolved the Cuban Missile Crisis by backing off and agreeing to remove U.S. missiles from Turkey, but facilitated future self-defeating machismo by pretending publicly that bluster and threats had done the trick. Had a single Soviet sailor named Vasily Arkhipov not refused to use a nuclear weapon, you might not be reading this. And yet there's always a higher level of madness still. In 1962's Operation Northwoods, proposed by the Joint Chiefs of Staff but rejected by Kennedy, the U.S. military proposed to have the CIA attack the United States and blame it on Cuba.

Up through today, the U.S. government has never ceased sabotaging Cuba, efforts that have taken a huge variety of forms, included numerous ridiculous assassination attempts and various not-funny-at-all bioweapon attacks, introducing swine fever to the island as well as tobacco mold, and creating "an epidemic of hemorrhagic dengue fever in 1981, during which some 340,000 people were infected and 116,000 hospitalized, this in a country which had never before experienced a single case of the disease. In the end, 158 people, including 101 children, died."[127]

Kennedy Doctrine

This doctrine is not always included in lists. When it is, it amounts to an update of the Monroe Doctrine for Latin America to involve the excluding, in particular, of the Soviet Union. This concept is cherry-picked out of President John F. Kennedy's inaugural address, in which he called for mass-participation in governance, committed to aiding the poor of the world, and didn't mention the Soviet Union but rather "aggression or subversion" in Latin America. In the same speech, but apparently unworthy of doctrine status, Kennedy urged support for the United Nations, for peace, and for reconciliation with enemies, while warning of the danger posed by nuclear weapons, and stating "Let both sides, for the first time, formulate serious

and precise proposals for the inspection and control of arms--and bring the absolute power to destroy other nations under the absolute control of all nations." Kennedy said the problems to tackle were "tyranny, poverty, disease, and war itself" and addressed himself to "citizens of the world," yet his "doctrine" is somehow an anti-Soviet Monroe Doctrine.[128]

The Cuban Revolution produced a great deal of talk in the U.S. of a need to restore the Monroe Doctrine. Here's the *New York Times* looking back from 1984, while claiming that the Monroe Doctrine had been largely forgotten during the 1970s:

> *"Edward V. Rickenbacker, World War I fighter ace and chairman of the board of Eastern Airlines, joined William F. Buckley Jr. in forming a Committee for the Monroe Doctrine to protest the Kennedy-Khrushchev agreement. Barry Goldwater and Richard Nixon advocated redefining and reinvoking the Doctrine. The New York State Conservative Party passed a resolution praising the Doctrine and calling for the ouster of the Communist regime in Cuba by whatever means necessary. The flurry of discussion of the Doctrine provoked by the Soviet presence in Cuba died away. In 1968, Soviet troops crushed a liberal regime in Czechoslovakia, and Premier Leonid Brezhnev justified the deed by saying that the Soviet Union had a right to intervene in the internal affairs of fraternal nations in order to defend the gains of Socialism. The fact that this policy instantly became known in the West as the 'Brezhnev Doctrine' indicated that a comparative allusion to the Monroe Doctrine was still recognizable."*[129]

For the most part, during the 1960s, the United States did not engage in military invasions of Latin America, but rather expanded its efforts to facilitate coups, and to arm, train, and try to control brutal governments. For example, between 1960 and 1963, the U.S. facilitated a successful coup attempt in Ecuador. The President of Ecuador was not a communist; he merely refused to be a rabid anti-communist, to cut ties with Cuba, to abuse the rights of leftist activists. The CIA went all out, creating phony parties and labor groups, paying off top officials, reading the mail, promoting propaganda, and getting its own man into power in 1961, and a more satisfactory replacement in 1963, upon which those identified by the CIA as communist were jailed, civil liberties suspended, and the planned 1964 elections called off.[130] The *New York Times* reported on the 1963 coup as if the United States had had nothing to do with it, as if the main failure of the man overthrown was drunkenness, and as if military coups were simply typical of the backward people of Latin America.[131]

From 1962 to 1964 the U.S. government also arranged for a coup in Brazil, the nation that, all the way back in 1940 had been the first in Latin America to sign a military staff agreement with the U.S. military. Brazilians trained at the U.S. National War College, and in 1949 established their own similar institution. As with many nations around the world, Brazil clashed with the U.S. over oil. In 1951 a former Brazilian dictator, Getúlio Vargas, tried out being a democratically elected president instead. The U.S. had no interest in that, it's "strategic national interest" was in Brazil's oil. The U.S. worked with the Escola Superior de Guerra to plot a coup, but it wasn't needed. Vargas tried to double the minimum wage, and Brazilian oligarchs overthrew him themselves. Yet they ended up with the originator of the minimum wage increase, João Goulart, as vice president, and eventually, in 1961, as president. In 1962 President Kennedy and the U.S. Ambassador to Brazil agreed to spend millions on defeating Goulart in that year's election, while planning a military coup as a back up. In March of 1964, Lyndon Johnson's U.S. government and the Brazilian military, pushing false accusations of communism, chased the president out of the country.[132]

On some occasions, even in countries where the United States had backed coups and dictators for decades, it opted for military invasions. One such occasion was 1965 in the Dominican Republic. President Lyndon Johnson was unable to sell a war to the U.S. public on Monroe Doctrine grounds, and opted instead to pretend that U.S. citizens were in danger. This was not a new excuse, and it's used to this day, as it would also be used with Grenada and Panama in the 1980s. In 1965 in the Dominican Republic, U.S. citizens who wanted to leave (1,856 of them) had been evacuated prior to the military action. Neighborhoods in Santo Domingo where Americans lived were free of violence and the military was not needed in order to evacuate anyone. All the major Dominican factions had agreed to help evacuate any foreigners who wanted to leave. That same year, President Johnson made his humanitarian and democratic motivations clear in a comment to the Greek ambassador:

> *"Fuck your parliament and your constitution. America is an elephant, Cyprus is a flea. If these two fleas continue itching the elephant, they may just get whacked by the elephant's trunk, whacked good. We pay a lot of good American dollars to the Greeks, Mr. Ambassador. If your Prime Minister gives me a talk about democracy, parliament, and constitutions, he, his parliament, and his constitution may not last very long."*[133]

Spreading democracy was not a top priority for the U.S. government in the 1960s and never has been, before or since. The military invasion of the Dominican Republic was aimed at keeping U.S. control of a Latin American nation, just the opposite of democracy.

Johnson Doctrine

The Johnson Doctrine is identical to the Kennedy one, and perhaps both more and less appropriately designated -- less because it was already Kennedy's, more because it was articulated by President Lyndon Johnson at the time of a U.S. war on the Dominican Republic, and again less because the false claim to be protecting the Dominican Republic from the Soviets was not prominently used by Johnson, as

he had determined that nobody was going to fall for it. Instead, Johnson principally used a false claim that U.S. citizens were in danger in the Dominican Republic, only followed secondarily by the justification of keeping communists out of the Western Hemisphere.[134] In a closed session of the Senate Foreign Relations Committee, Assistant Secretary of State Thomas Mann later explained that the U.S. ambassador had asked the head of the Dominican military if he'd be willing to play along with the alternative lie: "All we requested was whether he would be willing to change the basis for this from one of fighting communism to one of protecting American lives."[135]

U.S. military actions in the Western Hemisphere in the 1960s included:

1962 Cuba
1965 Dominican Republic

U.S.-backed coup attempts in the 1960s included:

Success in British Guiana 1953-64
Failure in Cuba 1959 to present
Success in Ecuador 1960-63
Success in Brazil 1962-64
Success in Dominican Republic 1963
Success in Bolivia 1964
Success in Chile 1964-73

In 1970, U.S. National Security Advisor Henry Kissinger, while failing to prevent the election of non-communist presidential candidate Salvador Allende in Chile, remarked: "I don't see why we need to stand by and watch a country go Communist due to the irresponsibility of its own people." President Richard Nixon told CIA director Richard Helms to "make the economy scream" in Chile. On September 11, 1973, Allende and many other people were murdered in a U.S.-backed coup that installed the horrific military dictatorship of Augusto Pinochet, who would stay in power through 1990, and from whose damage Chile would work to recover to this day.

Nixon Doctrine

On November 3, 1969, President Richard Nixon, said: "First, the United States will keep all of its treaty commitments. Second, we shall provide a shield if a nuclear power threatens the freedom of a nation allied with us or of a nation whose survival we consider vital to our security. Third, in cases involving other types of aggression, we shall furnish military and economic assistance when requested in accordance with our treaty commitments. But we shall look to the nation directly threatened to assume the primary responsibility of providing the manpower for its defense."[136] This was also referred to as the Vietnamization of the war on Vietnam. It advanced the practice, still current, and exemplified by the current war in Ukraine, or arming and training and funding the people of other countries to fight wars, while not deploying large number of U.S. troops. This twist on U.S. imperialism does little to reduce the risk of nuclear apocalypse, or the wasting of resources on weapons, or the death and suffering and environmental destruction of wars, but it does reduce the direct U.S. casualties, which at the time of the war on Vietnam and ever since has been key to determining the acceptability of wars to the U.S. public. The mechanization of wars with drones, the use of mercenary companies, and of course the substitution of the poverty draft for a formal draft, can be seen as falling into this tradition.

There's another "doctrine" that's not framed on the walls of imperial altars with presidential doctrines, but that has been in recent decades an increasingly important part of the Monroe Doctrine. I mean the Shock Doctrine, a name that comes from the title of a book by Naomi Klein, in which she recounts the far more extensive than usual planning and follow through that surrounded the 1973 Chilean coup, and the "shock" both of rapid economic destruction and of its enforcement through imprisonment, torture, and murder. Years before the coup, U.S. economist Milton Friedman, with the aid of the U.S. State Department and of the Ford Foundation, made the University of Chicago's radically rightwing economics department the top U.S. economics school for Latin American students. Between 1957 and 1970, U.S. tax payers and foundations gave 100 Chileans advanced degrees in economic devastation from the University of Chicago. In 1973, alumni of U.S. military training and these alumni of Friedman's economic training together seized power in Chile and imposed tax cuts, free trade, privatization, deregulation, and the elimination of public services, including of public schools.[137]

A similar combination of rapid and massive change imposed through violence in the 1970s saw Argentina "disappear" 30,000 people, most of them leftist activists, while establishing Chicago School policies as in Chile. The University of Chicago directly trained students from across Latin America, but also worked with alumni in Chile to set up schools in places like Argentina and Colombia for the indoctrination of what they called neoliberalism.

The phase of U.S.-facilitated abuse in Latin America that began in 1975 -- or much of it -- was given the name Operation Condor, after Chile's national bird. This was the name of an international death squad formed by the United States, Chile, and Brazil, as well as Argentina, Bolivia, Paraguay, and Uruguay, modeled in part on the 1965-begun efforts in Indonesia, where the CIA helped the Indonesian military kill approximately 1 million civilians and successfully move the country to the right and to U.S.-allegiance, without the attention, or the loss of U.S. military lives, or the abysmal failure of the war on Vietnam.[138] Operation Condor used U.S. computers to create an international list of communists and leftists to be murdered, and murdered some 60,000 to 80,000 of them during the 1970s and 1980s, while similar efforts were used around the globe, including in

Guatemala (200,000 killed from 1954 to 1996)
El Salvador (75,000 killed from 1979 to 1992)

Nicaragua (50,000 killed from 1979 to 1989)
Colombia (3,000 to 5,000 killed from 1985 to 1995)
Mexico (1300 killed from 1965 to 1982)
Venezuela (500 to 1,500 killed from 1959 to 1970)
Honduras (200 killed from 1980 to 1993)[139]

Since 1976, the International Covenant on Civil and Political Rights (ICCPR) and the International Covenant on Economic, Social, and Cultural Rights have bound their parties to these opening words of Article I of both treaties: "All peoples have the right of self-determination." U.S.-backed coup attempts in Latin America and the Caribbean in the 1970s included:

Failure in Costa Rica 1970-71
Success in Bolivia 1971
Success in Jamaica 1976-80

In 1975, we should note, a U.S. Senate select committee headed by Senator Frank Church investigated and exposed decades of crimes by the CIA and other parts of the U.S. government, including assassinations, torture, human experimentation, propaganda, warrantless spying, etc. This resulted in various weak reforms, including an executive order forbidding the murdering of foreign leaders, and a new court that would rubberstamp warrants for spying on the public. It also led to the creation of new agencies that would eventually do openly much of what the CIA had done secretly to support the overthrow of foreign governments. The National Endowment for Democracy (NED) would be set up in 1983.

The Church Committee's massive report includes a section on Chile that catalogued nefarious U.S. activities leading up to the 1973 coup, and introduced the topic with these words:

"In the same year that the United States recognized Chilean independence, 1823, it also proclaimed the Monroe Doctrine. This unilateral policy pronouncement of the United States was directed as a warning toward rival European powers not to interfere in the internal political affairs of this hemisphere. The U. S. reaction to Fidel Castro's rise to power suggested that while the Monroe Doctrine had been abandoned, the principles which prompted it were still alive. Castro's presence spurred a new United States hemispheric policy with special significance for Chile - the Alliance for Progress. There was little disagreement among policymakers either at the end of the Eisenhower Administration or at the beginning of the Kennedy Administration that something had to be done about the alarming threat that Castro was seen to represent to the stability of the hemisphere. The U.S. reaction to the new hemispheric danger - communist revolution - evolved into a dual policy response. Widespread malnutrition, illiteracy, hopeless housing conditions and hunger for the vast majority of Latin Americans who were poor; these were seen as communism's allies. Consequently, the US undertook loans to national development programs and supported civilian reformist regimes, all with an eye to preventing the appearance of another Fidel Castro in our hemisphere."

Well not all with an eye to that. Gifts would have been all with eye to that. Loans were something else. The report continued:

"But there was another component in U.S. policy toward Latin America. Counterinsurgency techniques were developed to combat urban or rural guerrilla insurgencies often encouraged or supported by Castro's regime. Development could not cure overnight the social ills which were seen as the breeding ground of communism. New loans for Latin American countries' internal national development programs would take time to bear fruit. In the meantime, the

communist threat would continue. The vicious circle plaguing the logic of the Alliance for Progress soon became apparent. In order to eliminate the short-term danger of communist subversion, it was often seen as necessary to support Latin American armed forces, yet frequently it was those same armed forces who were helping to freeze the status quo which the Alliance sought to alter."[140]

Carter Doctrine

On January 23, 1980, in his State of the Union address, President Jimmy Carter said, "Let our position be absolutely clear: An attempt by any outside force to gain control of the Persian Gulf region will be regarded as an assault on the vital interests of the United States of America, and such an assault will be repelled by any means necessary, including military force."[141] The U.S. already had doctrines globalizing the Monroe Doctrine, applying it specifically to the Middle East, and committing to war for the protection of oil. This one reinforced those.

The 1980s saw a bit of economic shock doctrine brought back to the United States and the United Kingdom by the Reagan and Thatcher governments, with a boost from the war crisis mentality surrounding a 10-week war between the UK and Argentina over the Falkland Islands / Islas Malvinas and nearby islands. These were islands off the coast of Argentina and nowhere near England, yet the British had long claimed them. When Argentina invaded and the British fought back, the U.S. government briefly tried to negotiate peace, and then backed the British -- just the opposite of what the basic thesis of the Monroe Doctrine might lead one to expect. Ironically, the inhabitants would have voted for British rule, being largely descendants of British sailors, and later did just that in 2013. Also ironically, the government of Argentina may have been moved in a positive direction by the unpopular military failure of losing this war. Sadly, the war madness and triumphalism in the UK did nothing to discourage Western militarism, which was still working to put the "Vietnam syndrome" behind it.

U.S. wars in Latin America in the 1980s included ones in Grenada in 1983, and Panama in 1989. In the case of Grenada (an invasion that the United States banned the U.S. media from covering) there were supposedly U.S. medical students to rescue. But U.S. State Department official James Budeit, two days before the invasion, learned that the students were not in danger. When about 100 to 150 students decided they wanted to leave, their reason was fear of the U.S. attack. The parents of 500 of the students sent President Ronald Reagan a telegram asking him not to attack, letting him know their children were safe and free to leave Grenada if they chose to do so. From the perspective of the 2020s it seems shameful for the United States to have used such transparent lies to market a war. But from the perspective of the long saga of the Monroe Doctrine, it seems positive that the U.S. government believed some story other than imperialism or adventurism or conquest was required. In this case, the Organisation of Eastern Caribbean States actually requested U.S. intervention. In the early years of the Monroe Doctrine such requests were more common and usually ignored. By the 1980s they were rare and deemed insufficient. By the 2020s they are virtually nonexistent in Latin America, desirable though they might be in certain quarters, with similar requests from other parts of the globe now serving as the primary propaganda justification for various wars (Ukraine, Syria, Saudi Arabia, etc.).

In the case of Panama in 1989, a real incident could be pointed to as a reason for war, one of a sort that has been found anywhere foreign armies have ever occupied someone else's country. Some drunk Panamanian soldiers had beaten up a U.S. navy officer and threatened his wife. While U.S. President George H. W. Bush claimed that this and other new developments prompted the war, the war plans had actually begun months prior to the incident.[142] Marlin Fitzwater, White House Press Secretary for Presidents Ronald Reagan and George H. W. Bush, said that war is "easier for people to understand if there's a face to the enemy." He gave examples: "Hitler, Ho Chi Minh, Saddam Hussein, Milosevic." Fitzwater might well have included the name Manuel Antonio Noriega. When the doctrineless first president Bush sought, among other things, to prove he was no "wimp" by attacking Panama in 1989, the most prominent justification was that Panama's leader was a mean, drug-crazed, weirdo with a pockmarked face who liked to commit adultery. An important article in the very serious *New York Times* on December 26, 1989, began:

> *"The United States military headquarters here, which has portrayed General Manuel Antonio Noriega as an erratic, cocaine-snorting dictator who prays to voodoo gods, announced today that the deposed leader wore red underwear and availed himself of prostitutes."*

Never mind that Noriega had worked for the CIA, including at the time he'd stolen the 1984 election in Panama. Never mind that his real offense was refusing to back a U.S.-backed war against Nicaragua. Never mind that the United States had known about Noriega's drug trafficking for years and continued working with him. This man snorted cocaine in red underwear with women not his wife. "That is aggression as surely as Adolf Hitler's invasion of Poland 50 years ago was aggression," declared Deputy Secretary of State Lawrence Eagleburger of Noriega's drug trafficking.[143] The invading U.S. liberators even claimed to find a big stash of cocaine in one of Noriega's homes, although it turned out to be tamales wrapped in banana leaves.

Which brings us to Central America. Death squads were employed there in the 1980s against popular movements to such an extent that similar tactics would be referred to in the 2020s in places like Iraq as "the Salvador Option" -- in part because the very same U.S. officials would be involved. Robert Parry reports:[144]

> *"The insurgencies in El Salvador and Guatemala were crushed through the slaughter of tens of thousands of civilians. In Guatemala, about 200,000 people perished, including what a truth commission*

later termed a genocide against Mayan Indians in the Guatemalan highlands. In El Salvador, about 70,000 died including massacres of whole villages, such as the slaughter carried out by a U.S.-trained battalion against hundreds of men, women and children in and around the town of El Mozote in 1981. The Reagan-Bush strategy also had a domestic component, the so-called 'perception management' operation that employed sophisticated propaganda to manipulate the fears of the American people while hiding the ugly reality of the wars. The Reagan-Bush administration justified its actions in Central America by portraying the popular uprisings as an attempt by the Soviet Union to establish a beachhead in the Americas to threaten the U.S. southern border."

When I attended Herndon High School in Herndon, Virginia, in the 1980s, one of my fellow students' fathers came in to speak to us, a man named Oliver North. He asked if we realized how close Nicaragua was, if we had any idea how afraid we should be that the communists were taking over a place that was virtually next-door to us. We would later see him on television testifying before Congress about criminal actions he had engaged in during the "Iran-Contra Scandal" -- testimony that much of the U.S. public seemed to believe made him a hero. It did later make him a talking head on the rightwing television channel Fox News.

Popular opposition to U.S.-backed dictatorship had been growing for years in Nicaragua. The U.S. government, right up through the Jimmy Carter administration, had sought to hold off a revolution that went under the name Sandinista. But the Sandinistas had taken over in 1979 with a clear agenda of not submitting to the dictates of the U.S. government or U.S.-dominated financial institutions like the IMF that were using debt to compel privatization and austerity around the globe. The Sandinistas began nationalization of Nicaraguan finances and trade, and the creation of a public sector, as well as agrarian reform, and tax reform.[145] Presidential candidate Ronald Reagan saw the Sandinistas as a major threat. Reagan had made a big deal of opposing President Carter's commitment to turn the Panama Canal over to Panama, and campaigned on nationalism, militarism, and rejection of concerns over human rights. Although the U.S. Congress would specifically forbid it, the Reagan administration would secretly train counter-revolutionary fighters (the "Contras") in Honduras for war in Nicaragua, and arm them with funds secretly and illegally raised through the sale of weapons to the supposed enemy of the United States, Iran.

In 1982, the *New York Times's* James Reston celebrated Ronald Reagan as a new supporter of the Monroe Doctrine.[146] In 1984, the Deputy Director of so-called Intelligence, Robert Gates -- later to be the CIA's Director and subsequently the Secretary of so-called Defense -- wrote a memo to then-CIA Director William Casey in which he stated his belief that merely assisting the Contras would not be enough, that U.S. warmaking was required, even if politically unacceptable, to defend the Monroe Doctrine:

> *"The alternative to our present policy--which I predict ultimately and inevitably is leading to the consolidation of the Nicaraguan regime and our facing a second Cuba in Central America--is overtly to try to bring down the regime. This involves a mustering of political force and will, first of all within the Administration, and second with the Congress, that we have not seen on any foreign policy issue (apart from our defense rearmament) in many years. It seems to me that this effort would draw upon the following measures: Withdrawal of diplomatic recognition of the regime in Managua and the recognition of a government in exile. Overt provision to the government in exile of military assistance, funds, propaganda support and so forth including major efforts to gain additional support in international community, including real pressure. Economic sanctions against Nicaragua, perhaps even including a quarantine. These sanctions would affect both exports and imports and would be combined*

with internal measures by the resistance to maximize the economic dislocation to the regime. Politically most difficult of all, the use of air strikes to destroy a considerable portion of Nicaragua's military buildup (focusing particularly on the tanks and the helicopters). This would be accompanied by an announcement that the United States did not intend to invade Nicaragua but that no more arms deliveries of such weapons would be permitted. These are hard measures. They probably are politically unacceptable. But it is time to stop fooling ourselves about what is going to happen in Central America. Putting our heads in the sand will not prevent the events that I outlined at the beginning of this note. Can the United States stand a second Cuba in the Western Hemisphere? One need only look at the difficulty that Cuba has caused this country over the past 25 years to answer that question. The fact is that the Western Hemisphere is the sphere of influence of the United States. If we have decided totally to abandon the Monroe Doctrine, if in the 1980's taking strong actions to protect our interests despite the hail of criticisms is too difficult, then we ought to save political capital in Washington, acknowledge our helplessness and stop wasting everybody's time."[147]

Reagan Doctrine

On April 1, 1985, pro-war Time magazine columnist Charles Krauthammer published a column called "The Reagan Doctrine" that created the Reagan Doctrine, citing but expanding on a passage from Reagan's 1985 State of the Union Address.[148] According to Krauthammer (a leading Iraq War liar in 2022-2003), "The Reagan Doctrine proclaims overt and unashamed American support for anti-Communist revolution. --200 years of American support for 'Simón Bolivar . . . the Polish patriots, the French Resistance and others seeking freedom.'" But of course, the U.S. government had been very slow to recognize the new nations of South America after they'd been established (as we'll see below), the Polish struggle against the Soviet Union was nonviolent[149], and the U.S. delayed invading France until years after it had been occupied. Never mind, Krauthammer was proclaiming U.S. support for violent revolutions to overthrow governments believed to be friendly to Russia. That Reagan

acted on this in Nicaragua in secret and in violation of various laws is in keeping with the general thrust of presidential doctrines, as they all support criminal activities, first and foremost the crime of war.[150] At the time of the Monroe Doctrine, U.S. government officials had been torn between believing that South American revolutions deserved support and believing that dark-skinned Catholics were incapable of self-governance, so perhaps some silver lining of ideological progress can be found in Krauthammer's wholehearted support for revolutions, at least to the extent that he wasn't planning on the U.S. running the resulting regimes.

While that Gates memo was private (for a short time), this was the era of the "Reagan Doctrine" publicly discussed. The U.S. government and punditry (or much of it, anyway) deemed Latin America worth caring about, in fact labeled it the top priority, and deemed Latin Americans capable of useful revolution -- as long as it was the rightwing counter-revolution of the Contras. Both houses of Congress in 1982 passed a resolution called the Symms Amendment declaring their intention to stop the spread of communism in the Western Hemisphere by "whatever means may be necessary . . . including use of arms." Senator Steven Symms' spokesperson described this as "a reinstitution of the Monroe Doctrine."[151] In 1984 the *New York Times* identified a brand new corollary that seems not to have stood the test of time, the Kissinger Corollary, named for Henry Kissinger who headed a commission that reported that Marxism-Leninism was a threat, not to Latin American democracy, and not to U.S. "interests," and not to U.S. "national security," but to the ability of the U.S. to intervene around the world. The U.S. would need to intervene against communism in Latin America to protect the U.S. ability to intervene elsewhere, at least without greater investment in "defense".[152]

Kissinger Corollary

Rarely mentioned, this was proposed in 1984 by the New York Times as a doctrine demanding the defense of Latin America against communism in order to maintain the ability to focus on intervening in the rest of the world.[153]

While the Weinberger Doctrine may have counseled restraint in certain cases (Vietnam or Lebanon), Secretary of "Defense" Caspar Weinberger favored action in Nicaragua in support of the Monroe Doctrine, and said so publicly before, during, and after the Iran-Contra Scandal.[154] President Reagan and his Ambassador to the United Nations Jeane Kirkpatrick maintained that the United States should not criticize rightwing governments, no matter how oppressive, because a leftwing totalitarian government might be the result. Reagan proceeded to support reactionary forces in Nicaragua, El Salvador, and elsewhere in Latin America.

Weinberger Doctrine

"The Weinberger Doctrine, named in honor of Reagan's Secretary of Defense, declares it is the policy of the United States to use its military forces only in the defense of American vital interests."[155] This one is rarely mentioned, presumably because no president's name can be attached to it, the U.S. government has never acted on it, and it runs counter to the whole idea of doctrines by limiting rather than expanding global violence.

The idea that this was a Monroe Doctrine defense of Nicaragua and El Salvador, despite consisting of violent attacks against supporters of majority views in those countries is based on the idea that the Soviet Union was trying to take over. And that idea was based in part on a false history of the Cuban Revolution, in which the Soviet Union had initiated it, rather than having been an ally of last resort when the United States had made its opposition clear. The idea of a Soviet takeover in Central America was also based in part on claims of Soviet influence and weapons in Nicaragua and El Salvador, claims that even the U.S. State Department deemed "exaggerated,"[156] but which were advanced through a special inter-agency office called the Office of Public Diplomacy for Latin America and the Caribbean.[157] This office put out made-up stories that Soviet fighter jets and chemical weapons were arriving in Nicaragua, that the Sandinistas were dealing drugs, that U.S. journalists (those deemed insufficiently critical of

Sandinistas by the Reagan White House) were being given sexual favors by the Sandinistas, and so forth.

The Monroe Doctrine had still never become, as it never would, what it had claimed to be, a defense against real and malign intervention from outside the hemisphere in defense of more democratic and independent nations of America. But as a rhetorical basis for intervening against democratic tendencies, it was alive and well. When the World Court in 1986 ordered the U.S. government to pay reparations to Nicaragua for the crime of mining its harbors, the U.S. simply ignored it, and has ever since. The Iran-Contra Scandal resulted in very little in the way of accountability for those involved, with Congress disinclined to oppose this particular sort of lawlessness, and much of the U.S. media and public inclined to cheer for it. In 1987, rightwing radical Phyllis Schlafly published a celebratory report on a U.S. State Department event celebrating the Monroe Doctrine:[158]

> *"A group of distinguished persons from the North American continent gathered in the U.S. State Department Diplomatic Rooms on April 28, 1987 to proclaim the lasting vitality and relevance of the Monroe Doctrine. It was an event of political, historical and social importance. Grenada's Prime Minister Herbert A. Blaize told how grateful his country is that Ronald Reagan used the Monroe Doctrine to liberate Grenada in 1983. Prime Minister Eugenia Charles of Dominica reinforced this gratitude. . . Secretary of State George Shultz told of the threat to the Monroe Doctrine posed by the Communist regime in Nicaragua, and he urged us to hold fast to the policy that bears Monroe's name. Then he unveiled to the public a magnificent Rembrandt Peale portrait of James Monroe, which has been privately held until now by Monroe's descendants. 'Monroe Doctrine' awards were presented to opinion makers whose words and actions 'support the continuing validity of the Monroe Doctrine.'"*

Schlafly explained that the Monroe Doctrine justified taking action to prevent communism, regardless of any threat from abroad:

> *"The Monroe Doctrine was never limited to preventing territorial aggression. The key word is 'system' – it prohibits extending the 'system' of Russia or other European powers to the Western Hemisphere. . . . [T]he Monroe Doctrine is not only part of our national heritage, it is part of our national honor. That's the same reason why the American people supported President Reagan's dramatic rescue of Grenada so overwhelmingly. The Symms Amendment, passed by big majorities in Congress in 1982 and again in 1984, reaffirms our commitment to the Monroe Doctrine. President Reagan recognized this in his 1987 State of the Union Message when he reminded us that his commitment to stop Communism in the Western Hemisphere did not start by spontaneous generation on the day he took office. 'It began,' he said, 'with the Monroe Doctrine in 1823 and continues today as our historic bipartisan American policy.' . . . The posh audience at the State Department dinner in April 1987 applauded vigorously when reminded that a good model for support of the Contras in their fight to win back freedom in Nicaragua occurred in 1954 when President Dwight Eisenhower authorized American support for an anti-Communist force which overthrew a Communist regime in Guatemala. . . . Nicaragua presents Americans with the choice: American -style freedom or Soviet-backed tyranny. The Monroe Doctrine still is the lamp by which our policy should be guided."*

U.S. opposition to the Sandinistas never ended, and when a new government was elected in 1990 it was with intimidation and violence by the Contras as well as a U.S. promise to end an embargo if its chosen candidate were elected.[159] U.S. military actions in the Western Hemisphere in the 1980s included:

1981 El Salvador
1981-1989 Nicaragua
1983 Grenada
1986 Bolivia
1988 Panama
1989 Bolivia
1989 Colombia
1989 Peru
1989-1990 Panama

U.S.-backed coup attempts in the 1980s included:

Success in Grenada 1983
Success in Nicaragua 1981-90
Success in Panama 1989

These lists are always potentially incomplete, due to secrecy, lies, and propaganda, but also due to the difficulty in drawing a line between coups involving and not involving U.S. support. If coups participated in by people who were once trained by the United States were our guide, then our lists of U.S.-backed coups would need to be significantly expanded. A lot of what we know about U.S. training of Latin Americans in war, torture, and assassination is thanks to an activist organization called the School of the Americas Watch, named in 1990 for the (later renamed) School of the Americas training academy at the U.S. military's Fort Benning in Georgia, begun as the Latin American Training Center-Ground Division in 1946 in the Panama Canal Zone, and moved to Fort Benning in 1984, renamed in 2001 the Western Hemisphere Institute for Security Cooperation. Over the years, the school has graduated tens of thousands of students from Latin America, including death squad members, coup leaders, torturers, assassins, and dictators:

- Argentine Junta leaders Emilio Massera and Jorge Rafael Videla Redondo, dictator General Roberto Viola, and dictator Leopoldo Galtieri.
- Bolivian coup leader Luis Arce Gomez, dictator Hugo Banzer Suarez, and torturer Urzagaste Rodriguez.
- And so on through the alphabet of nations.[160]

Training manuals used by the School of the Americas, as by the U.S. military, have long included torture. The School of the Americas has taught extortion, censorship, false arrest, execution and the "neutralizing" of enemies.[161] The notion that this outrage has all been dealt with and no longer continues is refuted by the latest posts on the School of the Americas Watch website. In 2022 a Honduran court convicted an alumnus of the murder of environmental activist Berta Caceres.[162] In 2021 four graduates were arrested for the assassination of the President of Haiti.[163] In 2019 a Bolivian graduate and head of the Bolivian military "suggested" that the President of Bolivia resign.[164] And so on.

Powell Doctrine

"The Powell Doctrine states that military force should only be used to win an overwhelming victory in a short period of time."[165] While President George H.W. Bush lacks a doctrine, his Chairman of the Joint Chiefs of Staff Colin Powell has a quasi-doctrine that was not acted on by his Commander in Chief, nor by himself when he later performed his Iraq war lies skit at the United Nations to sell an endless occupation of Iraq to U.S. television viewers -- having already been warned by his own staff that his claims would not even sound plausible[166]. His later and related Pottery Barn Doctrine has perhaps never been called a doctrine but should be if only to highlight the dumbness of doctrines.[167]

One doctrine heavily advanced by the Bill Clinton administration in the 1990s was that of "free trade" -- free only if you're not considering damage to the environment, workers' rights, or independence from large multinational corporations. The United States wanted, and perhaps still wants, one big free trade agreement for all nations in the Americas except Cuba and perhaps others identified for exclusion. What it got in 1994 was NAFTA, the North American Free Trade Agreement, binding the United States, Canada, and Mexico to its terms. This would be followed in 2004 by CAFTA-DR, the Central America - Dominican Republic Free Trade Agreement among the United States, Costa Rica, the Dominican Republic, El Salvador, Guatemala, Honduras, and Nicaragua, which would be followed by numerous other agreements and attempts at agreements, including the TPP, Trans-Pacific Partnership for nations bordering the Pacific, including in Latin America; thus far the TPP has been defeated by its unpopularity within the United States. George W. Bush proposed a Free Trade Area of the Americas at a Summit of the Americas in 2005, and saw it defeated by Venezuela, Argentina, and Brazil.[168]

Clinton Doctrine

There seems to be agreement that President Bill Clinton must have a doctrine, but not on what it is. It's either a sort of broken-windows global policing, where the global cop proactively jumps in to deal with any incipient problem. Or it's a commitment to fight wars against genocide, as if war were not genocide and genocide not war. Or it's corporate trade agreements. The biggest impact on war justifications to have come out of the Clinton era seems to be an argument that there should have been a war in Rwanda to prevent a massacre. This war that didn't happen but supposedly should have is one of the more common examples people give when asked for examples of just wars other than World War II.[169] Developing later out of this line of thinking was the global doctrine of "Responsibility to Protect." This is all very much in the tradition of the Roosevelt Corollary.

NAFTA and its children have brought big benefits to big corporations, including U.S. corporations moving production to Mexico and Central America in the hunt for lower wages, fewer workplace rights, and weaker environmental standards. They've created commercial ties, but not social or cultural ties. They've harmed workers, farmers, and the environment.[170] The United States had about 20 million manufacturing jobs before NAFTA, and lost about 5 million of them, including the closure of more than 60,000 facilities. Mexico and other Latin American nations have been made ever more dependent on U.S. corporations. There have been powerful responses, such as the Zapatista uprising. But the largest impact may have been the empowerment of corporations to trade, invest, and divest as they like, to move in and behave as they see fit while holding out the threat to leave again at a moment's notice should any inconvenient standards be imposed on their behavior that might be avoided in some other corner of the globe. Beyond that, these treaties empower corporations to sue governments in non-governmental tribunals over standards they find inconvenient. Corporations have, through lawsuits and the threat thereof, been able to force the opening of various territories to mining and to effective colonial control.[171]

In Honduras today, highly unpopular "zones of employment and economic development" are maintained by U.S. pressure but also by U.S.-based corporations suing the Honduran government under CAFTA.[172] The result is a new form of filibustering or banana republic, in which the ultimate power rests with profiteers, the U.S. government largely but somewhat vaguely supports the pillaging, and the victims are mostly unseen and unimagined -- or when they show up at the U.S. border are blamed. As shock doctrine implementers, the corporations governing "zones" of Honduras, outside of Honduran law, are able to impose laws ideal to their own profits -- profits so excessive that they are easily able to pay U.S.-based think tanks to publish justifications as democracy for what is more or less democracy's opposite.

Popular protests opposed agreements like CAFTA before they were created, accurately predicting that they would throw farmers off the land by allowing multinational corporations to dump surplus crops at below-market prices, cause poverty, spread pollution, and lead to large numbers of people trying to flee to the United States from the devastation being imposed on their homes by U.S. corporations.[173]

Of course commercial power is somewhat distinct from U.S. government power, although its role in the utilization of the Monroe Doctrine has been a major one from the start. But with the United States cutting back on military invasions, and with U.S. corporate media doctrine treating the spreading of corporate power as not only desirable but inevitable, it is possible to imagine that the use and abuse of the Monroe Doctrine had begun receding. President Clinton hosted a "Summit of the Americas" meeting of OAS states in 1994. All might appear respectful diplomacy. But the supposedly inevitable and beneficial spread of global trade was one-sided. The idea that a Honduran corporation might own and rule, say, North Dakota or Kentucky would be properly treated as an outrage. And of course the United States excluded Cuba from the OAS, backed a military coup in 2000 in Ecuador, and continued openly using force to exclude self-governance from Haiti.

From 1957 to 1986, the United States armed and supported a family dictatorship in Haiti, after which it armed the Haitian military and funded its chosen electoral candidates. Nonetheless, popular supporter of Haitian self-governance Jean-Bertrand Aristide took power in February 1991 following a decisive electoral victory. Within eight months he was overthrown by a military coup backed by CIA- and NED-supported elements. After over three years of accepting the coup government, the U.S. military used the restoration of Aristide, as it has used various natural disasters over the years, as an excuse to invade Haiti -- the U.S. government having meanwhile pressured Aristide to abandon his earlier positions on independence and ending poverty (which he arguably only scaled back and did not abandon), and to agree not to serve as president the time he had been exiled by the coup.[174] Out of office in 1996, Aristide would be elected again in 2000. In 2003 he would demand that France pay back the funds it had collected from Haiti as compensation for the loss of property, including human beings, in the Haitian revolution. In 2004 he would be forced into exile again by another coup with U.S. involvement. A United Nations "stabilisation" mission in Haiti from 2004 to 2017 was designed to keep Aristide and his Lavalas party out of power. "The U.S.," Brian Concannon tells me, "is now supporting a deeply corrupt, repressive, unconstitutional government, and trying to organize another intervention, precisely to keep Lavalas out of power."

With the Monroe Doctrine far from dead and buried, U.S. President George W. Bush arrived in 2001 as yet another reviver of it, mainly through harsher rhetoric and clumsier coup attempts. But Bush the Second was given his own doctrine by the U.S. corporate media, which amounted to the doctrine of launching major horrific wars under a variety of evolving excuses with a minor role played by a pretense of spreading democracy. These wars were outside of Latin America, and -- as with the U.S. Civil War, and perhaps World War II -- they may have given Latin America a bit of breathing room.

Bush Doctrine

Again promoted by Charles Krauthammer, this doctrine, named for President George W. Bush, is generally considered to include opposition to international law, and the launching of major wars against distant nations with claims of policing terrorism. Like every other doctrine, this one is a variation on a steady theme, its seeds discernable in the original Monrovian claim to make various parts of the world into legitimate battlegrounds for U.S. wars.

An independence-minded president, Hugo Chavez, took power in Venezuela in 1999. In 2002, Bush used veterans of Iran-Contra crimes in an unsuccessful attempt to overthrow Chavez.[175] The U.S. went on to unsuccessfully attempt coups in Venezuela in 2018, 2019, and 2020. As of today, U.S. media outlets and websites like Wikipedia treat a man never elected as president, who has never served as president of Venezuela, the U.S.-educated and U.S.-directed Juan Guaidó, as having been president of Venezuela since 2019. This is at least a new twist: treating an unsuccessful coup as if it had succeeded. But coups have become embarrassing exceptions to other forms of pressure, many of them financial (debt, "aid," sanctions), some of them even quieter (the co-opting of elites, the training of fighters), some of them military but funded directly by U.S. corporations. In 2007, for example, Chiquita Brands pleaded guilty in U.S. court to aiding and abetting a terrorist organization, which is to say a group taking part in a decade-long civil war in Colombia, as well as in attacks on labor organizers. But the U.S. government refused to extradite individuals involved to stand trial in Colombia.

McClatchy Newspapers declared that the Monroe Doctrine had died (yet again) during the George W. Bush years, as Venezuela had elected a president who defied U.S. directives, and numerous Latin American nations traded and made trade agreements with nations in Europe and Asia, as well as with Canada, (building on U.S.-created corporate trade agreements to further empower, not the U.S. government, but corporations).[176] But who would have lamented any of that, had the Monroe Doctrine actually been dead? Wasn't media concern for the monopolization of trade and the control of Latin American governments by U.S. business interests proof that for the creators of the Monroe Doctrine, namely U.S. media outlets, it was alive and kicking?

U.S. military actions in the Western Hemisphere in the 1990s and 2000s included:

1993-1996 Haiti

2000-2016 Colombia

2004 Haiti

U.S.-backed coup attempts in the 2000s included:

Success in Ecuador 2000
Failure in Venezuela 2002
Success in Haiti 2004
Success in Honduras 2009

Latin American elections increasingly went against subservience to U.S. power. Following Hugo Chavez's "Bolivarian revolution," Néstor Carlos Kirchner was elected in Argentina in 2003, and Luiz Inácio Lula da Silva in Brazil in 2003. Independence-minded President of Bolivia Evo Morales took power in January 2006. Independence-minded President of Ecuador Rafael Correa came into power in January 2007. Correa announced that if the United States wished to keep a military base any longer in Ecuador, then Ecuador would have to be permitted to maintain its own base in Miami, Florida.[177] Correa has to this day denounced the ongoing U.S. use of the Monroe Doctrine.[178] In Nicaragua, Sandinista leader Daniel Ortega, ousted in 1990, has been back in power from 2007 to today, though clearly his policies have changed and his abuses of power are not all fabrications of the U.S. media. Andrés Manuel López Obrador (AMLO) was elected in Mexico in 2018. After set-backs, including a coup in Bolivia in 2019 (with U.S. and UK support -- completely in line with the actual history, if not the rhetoric, of the Monroe Doctrine) and a trumped-up prosecution in Brazil, 2022 saw the list of "pink tide" governments enlarged to include Venezuela, Bolivia, Ecuador, Nicaragua, Brazil, Argentina, Mexico, Peru, Chile, Colombia, and Honduras. For Colombia, 2022 saw its first election of a left-leaning president ever.[179] For Honduras, 2021 saw the election as president of the former first lady Xiomara Castro de Zelaya who had been ousted by the 2009 coup against her husband and now first gentleman Manuel Zelaya. These elections meant restoration of relations with Venezuela.

Of course, these countries are full of differences, as are their governments and presidents. Of course those governments and presidents are deeply flawed, as are all governments on Earth whether or not U.S. media outlets exaggerate or lie about their flaws. Nonetheless, Latin American elections (and resistance to coup attempts) suggest a trend in the direction of Latin America ending the Monroe Doctrine, whether the United States likes it or not.

The 2019 coup in Bolivia used the OAS to promote lies about election flaws, in order to paint a coup as an effort to protect democracy. This seems to be an increasingly popular model, preferred to that of the 2009 coup in Honduras, but even that was disguised as an election, albeit one that most of the world did not recognize.[180] The U.S. supported coups disguised as elections or legal actions in Paraguay in 2012 and Brazil in 2016 as well.[181] In Honduras, following the 2009 coup, the U.S. supported the coup government and new elections that were held under dramatically unfair conditions that produced the post-coup government that lasted until 2021.

Two writers at the Institute for Policy Studies asked U.S. President Barack Obama in 2009 to end the Monroe Doctrine. He did not. But in 2013, purely rhetorically, U.S. Secretary of State John Kerry announced to the OAS that "the era of the Monroe Doctrine is over."

Obama Doctrine

There is agreement that Obama must have a doctrine, but not on what it is. It is either challenging China as a threat to U.S. domination of the globe, or it is using less militarism than Bush, or it is an undefined middle path between peacemaking and warmaking. The Obama-era innovation of wars fought entirely with robotic flying airplanes seems not to have achieved status as a doctrine nominee. During Obama's presidency, Vice President Joe Biden played a role in foreign policy, mainly keeping the war on Iraq going as long as possible and the war on Afghanistan going right into the next presidency and beyond (to finally be ended when Biden himself was president), and there was talk of a "Biden Doctrine" but not a clear articulation of what it was.

The next U.S. president to bring the Monroe Doctrine back from a grave it had never even gone near was Donald Trump. The U.S. government's desire to overthrow Venezuela has been fairly constant since before the Trump presidency and continuing after it. But Trump, more than other presidents, tended to blurt out what he was thinking, including contemplating military action.[182] CIA Director Mike Pompeo, who publicly admitted that lying was a big part of what he did at the CIA, gave an attack on Venezuela a Monroe Doctrine spin by claiming that problems in Venezuela were caused by Cuba, Russia, Iran, and Hezbollah.[183] Venezuela presented the United Nations with a list of 27 damaging U.S. interventions in Latin America that it considered implementations of the Monroe Doctrine. In the George W. Bush tradition, Trump went in for blatancy and incompetence in adding to that list.

In 2019, anyone near a U.S. television or newspaper learned that the government of Venezuela needed to be overthrown because it wouldn't allow delivery of humanitarian aid. The story was false. The U.S. government had imposed brutal sanctions on Venezuela for years, resulting in at least 40,000 deaths at that point, and had sought to cut off electricity.[184] There were many places on Earth in desperate need of humanitarian aid. Venezuela was in fact busy allowing in tons of humanitarian aid (needed largely because of U.S. sanctions) from any nation or agency not attempting to overthrow the Venezuelan government.[185] Venezuela had a good reason not to let in U.S. aid. The U.S. government was apparently trying to ship weapons with which to take over Venezuela — an overthrow that the U.S. National Security Advisor shamelessly said would be on behalf of U.S. oil companies.[186]

U.S. weapons-funded think tanks urged war to uphold the Monroe Doctrine.[187] U.S. corporate media outlets seemed either unaware of the U.S. sanctions or eager to support them, falsely reported that Juan Guaidó had been elected president, falsely reported that Venezuelan forces blocked humanitarian aid and burned aid trucks (actually burned by coup proponents), falsely reported that Guaidó had taken over an airport, and failed to acknowledge the illegality of overthrowing governments or even to recall Donald Trump's acknowledgement prior to entering the White House that such actions tend to be disastrous.[188]

Trump and his cabinet members and advisors openly proclaimed their support for the Monroe Doctrine. But before, during, and after those years, an extreme bipartisan consensus, if not unanimous agreement, prevailed in the U.S. Congress that the top priority in all matters was competing with China -- with competition blurring into the possibility of eventual war. So, while it may now be acceptable to reject the Monroe Doctrine, the idea of dismissing concerns over Chinese influence in the Western Hemisphere is almost unthinkable, and for many that's simply an application of the Monroe Doctrine.

Trump Doctrine

The Trump Doctrine is either brilliant or horrendous, depending on whether you're speaking with a Trump follower or not, but either way it exists and has something to do with lacking or disregarding knowledge and information in order to treat foreign relations as business deals, openly opposing the United States to the rest of the world, and despising foreigners while claiming wars are stupid, even while keeping the war on Afghanistan going. Mostly, it seems to have a lot to do with the idea that every clown who holds the presidency must have a doctrine.

For centuries now a great way to criticize a political enemy in the United States has been to claim that everyone but them abides by the sacred Monroe Doctrine. In 2017, Congressman French Hill did a little mythmaking in the *Dallas Morning News*, writing, in part:[189]

> *"For two centuries, since President James Monroe's caution to the European powers, America has offered the Western Hemisphere a*

beacon of hope and reminder of independence. President Monroe's enduring Monroe Doctrine has served for successive presidents as the building block of our foreign policy, insisting upon resistance to hostile, intrusive actions in the Western Hemisphere, thus preserving order and democracy in our half of the globe.... Ultimately, Reagan's policies ushered in one of the great waves of democracy in Latin America during the 1980's. The actions by both Reagan and Clinton enhanced American prestige in the region.... Despite having many global priorities, President Bush enhanced economic growth and security in the Western Hemisphere by opening up Colombia to greater U.S. exports and contributing to Colombian President Alvaro Uribe's historic defeat of the FARC and diminishment of narcoterrorism. Like his predecessor, President Barack Obama faced geopolitical challenges, such as wars in Iraq and Afghanistan, a reemerging Russian aggression, and Chinese provocation in Southeast Asia. But, unlike those before him, he failed to lead in our hemisphere, and where he did engage, his efforts were ill-conceived. As his attention was drawn from our neighborhood to those elsewhere, Obama saw to the diminishment of the robust Monroe Doctrine, culminating in then-Secretary of State John Kerry's 2013 declaration that the Monroe Doctrine was dead."

U.S.-backed coup attempts in Latin America in recent years have included:

Success in Bolivia in 2019
Failure in Venezuela in 2018, 2019, 2020

When Joe Biden replaced Donald Trump as U.S. President in 2021, the main change in terms of the Monroe Doctrine was that U.S. officials stopped talking about it. Some of them even began talking about ceasing to blame immigrants and turning instead to assisting Latin American nations in creating places people would be happy to live in and not need to flee. But the main problem for over two centuries was never an inability to think of what the decent thing to do would be. And saying it out loud only gets us so far, if words are not followed by actions. Unfortunately, the Biden administration is continuing to advance the interests of oversized corporations, and not those of most workers, meaning that its effort to address the root causes of migration are likely to be counterproductive, and predictably and familiarly so.[190]

Biden Doctrine

Journalists are currently competing to create the Biden Doctrine. The leading contender is probably the claim to be pitting "rules based democracies" against autocracies and law violators, or in other words, opposing Russia and China all over the world. This is a clear continuation of Monroe Doctrine themes, including the theme of hypocrisy.

The first step in trying to actually do good ought to be to cease actively doing harm, and in this case that ought to begin with a complete moratorium on supporting coups. As I write this, we don't have that. The U.S. government supports actual coup governments as well as a pretend one, not really in power, in Venezuela. As I write, Peru is in turmoil, churning through its seventh president in six years under a constitution that facilitates such turnover, a constitution established under U.S.-backed dictator Alberto Fujimori. His daughter, Keiko Fujimori, has worked with people with connections to the CIA while leading the successful effort to unseat President Pedro Castillo.[191] In Argentina, judges have barred Vice President Cristina Fernández de Kirchner from ever again holding public office. She had been senator, first lady, and president, and might run for president again if the ruling is overturned. In 2022, President Biden renewed an executive order made by President Trump that ridiculously but menacingly declares Nicaragua to be an "unusual and extraordinary threat to the national security and foreign policy of the United States."

A positive note, standing in stark contrast to much U.S. history in Brazil and Latin America, was struck in 2022, when the U.S. Senate passed a resolution opposing any effort to overturn the fair results of a presidential election in Brazil, where the right-wing incumbent had threatened to challenge unfavorable results. The U.S. Senate threatened, of all things, to withhold aid from Brazil if there were a coup. Senator Bernie Sanders commented: "[President] Bolsonaro, an open admirer of the former U.S.-backed 1964-85 military dictatorship in whose army he served as an officer, has warned he may not accept the results of the election in the likely event he loses."[192]

Consistently taking that sort of stand would make a great difference, but would not immediately undo the structures that have been put in place over 200 years and more. By structures, I mean U.S. military bases, U.S.-supplied weapons, U.S.-trained troops and police and prison guards, corporate trade agreements, financial debts, and sanctions. The U.S. military maintains bases or the use of local bases in Puerto Rico, Panama, Honduras, El Salvador, Colombia, Cuba, Curaçao, and elsewhere, with many more nearby in Texas and in Florida where the U.S. maintains a command center that claims to command the hemisphere. The U.S. even has use of an island in the middle of the South Atlantic called Ascension Island that the British used in the Falklands war. Colombia has been made a NATO partner, despite not being near the North Atlantic. The United States supplies weapons to almost every Latin American government, as well as personnel to maintain, update, and train on them. Many U.S. weapons are manufactured from materials extracted from Latin America. The U.S. military provides training and funding to most Latin American militaries.[193] Undoing all of that would take a serious initiative, not just a press release, and right now it's hardly even comprehended as any sort of problem.

Similarly, the corporate trade agreements, debt repayment agreements, and sanctions are in place. The U.S. government would have to work to undo those things, assuming the corporations would even permit it. The United States has in place unilateral sanctions illegally punishing whole populations in dozens of countries around the world including Cuba, Haiti, Nicaragua, Paraguay, and Venezuela. Every year, at the United Nations, every nation on Earth votes to end the U.S. sanctions against Cuba, but two nations vote No: Israel and the United States, the latter of which of course has veto power in the absurdly undemocratic Security Council.

In 2013 Gallup conducted polls in Argentina, Mexico, Brazil, and Peru, and in each case found the United States the top answer to "What country is the greatest threat to peace in the world?"[194] In 2017, Pew conducted polls in Mexico, Chile, Argentina, Brazil, Venezuela, Colombia, and Peru, and found between 56% and 85% believing the United States to be a threat to their country.[195] If the Monroe Doctrine is either gone or benevolent, why haven't any of the people impacted by it heard about that?

Tied up with the use of the Monroe Doctrine in Latin America is the question of immigration. The blaming and demonization of immigrants into the United States serves as a distraction from useful politics, but also as a means of generating distance if not hostility toward Latin American nations. Immigrants themselves, on balance, help, within the United States, to generate pressure for more humane policies toward Latin America. The same corporate interests that have long sought to exploit workers south of the United States have also long sought to bring workers without rights into the United States to be exploited. Of course, I'd like to see both a transformation of U.S. foreign policy to benefit Latin America and open welcoming borders for anyone seeking to move. But currently, with so many people indoctrinated with the blaming of immigrants, it may be useful to persuade some of them to seek to address the root causes of immigration, just as President Joe Biden has pretended to do.

6. *What Has Been Built on Its Foundations?*

This is a partial list of U.S. military actions with those in the Western Hemisphere in bold but others around the world included (not including a much longer list of foreign military actions armed, trained, and advised by the United States):[196]

1840 Fiji Islands

1841 Samoa

1841 Tabiteuea

1842 Mexico

1843 China

1844 Mexico

1846-1848 Mexico

1847-1850 Cayuse

1849 Turkey

1850-1886 Apache

1851 Johanna Island

1851 Turkey

1852-1853 Argentina

1853-1854 Japan

1853-1854 Nicaragua

1853-1854 Ryukyu, Ogasawara islands

1854-1856 China

1855 Fiji Islands

1855 Uruguay

1855-1856 Rogue River Indigenous Peoples

1855-1856 Yakima, Walla Walla, Cayuse

1855-1858 Seminole

1856 Panama (Colombia)

1856-1857 Cheyenne

1857 Nicaragua

1858 Coeur d'Alene Alliance

1858 Fiji Islands

1858 Uruguay

1858-1859 Turkey

1859 China

1859 Mexico

1859 Paraguay

1860 Angola

1860 Colombia

1862 Sioux

1863-1864 Japan

1864 Cheyenne

1865 Panama (Colombia)

1866 China

1866 Mexico

1866-1868 Lakota Sioux, Northern Cheyenne, Northern Arapaho

1867 Formosa (Taiwan)

1867 Nicaragua

1867-1875 Comanche

1868 Colombia

1868 Japan

1868 Uruguay

1870 Hawaii

1871 Korea

1872-1873 Modoc

1873 Colombia (Panama)

1873-1896 Mexico

1874 Hawaii

1874-1875 Comanche, Apache, Arapaho, Cheyenne, Kiowa

1876-1877 Sioux

1877 Nez Perce

1878 Bannock (Banna'kwut)

1878-1879 Cheyenne

1879-1880 Utes

1882 Egypt

1885 Panama (Colombia)

1888 Haiti

1888 Korea

1888-1889 Samoa

1889 Hawaii

1890 Argentina

1890 Lakota Sioux

1891 Bering Straight

1891 Chile

1891 Haiti

1893 Hawaii

1894 Brazil

1894 Nicaragua

1894-1895 China

1894-1896 Korea

1895 Panama (Colombia)

1896 Nicaragua

1898 Cuba (Spain)

1898 Nicaragua

1898 Philippines (Spain)

1898 Puerto Rico (Spain)

1898-1899 China

1899 Nicaragua

1899 Samoa

1899-1913 Philippines

1900 China

1901-1902 Colombia

1903 Dominican Republic

1903 Honduras

1903 Syria

1903-1904 Abyssinia (Ethiopia)

1903-1914 Panama

1904 Dominican Republic

1904 Tangier

1904-1905 Korea

1906-1909 Cuba

1907 Honduras

1909-1910 Nicaragua

1911-1912 Honduras

1911-1914 China

1912 Cuba

1912 Turkey

1912-1933 Nicaragua

1914 Dominican Republic

1914 Haiti

1914-1919 Mexico

1915-1934 Haiti

1916-1924 Dominican Republic

1917-1918 World War I (Europe)

1917-1922 Cuba

1918-1920 Russia

1918-1921 Panama

1919 Dalmatia

1919 Turkey

1919-1920 Honduras

1925 Panama

1932 El Salvador

1941-1945 World War II (Europe, North Africa, Asia/Pacific)

1946 Trieste

1947-1949 Greece

1948-1949 Berlin, Germany

1950 Formosa (Taiwan)

1950-1953 Korea

1953-1954 Formosa (Taiwan)

1955-1975 Vietnam

1956 Egypt

1958 Lebanon

1962 Cuba

1962 Thailand

1962-1975 Laos

1964 Congo (Zaire)

1965 Dominican Republic

1965-1973 Cambodia

1967 Congo (Zaire)

1976 Korea

1978 Congo (Zaire)

1980 Iran

1981 El Salvador

1981 Libya

1981-1989 Nicaragua

1982-1983 Egypt

1982-1983 Lebanon

1983 Chad

1983 Grenada

1986 Bolivia

1986 Libya

1987-1988 Iran

1988 Panama

1989 Bolivia

1989 Colombia

1989 Libya

1989 Peru

1989 Philippines

1989-1990 Panama

1990 Saudi Arabia

1991 Congo (Zaire)

1991-1992 Kuwait

1991-1993 Iraq

1992-1994 Somalia

1993-1994 Macedonia

1993-1996 Haiti

1993-2005 Bosnia

1995 Serbia

1996 Liberia

1996 Rwanda

1997-2003 Iraq

1998 Afghanistan

1998 Sudan

1999-2000 Kosovo

1999-2000 Montenegro

1999-2000 Serbia

2000 Yemen

2000-2002 East Timor

2000-2016 Colombia

2001-2021 Afghanistan

2001- Pakistan

2001- Somalia

2002-2015 Philippines

2002- Yemen

2003-2011 Iraq

2004 Haiti

c2004- Kenya

2011 Democratic Republic of the Congo

2011-2017 Uganda
2011- Libya
c2012- Central African Republic
c2012- Mali
c2013-2016 South Sudan
c2013- Burkina Faso
c2013- Chad
c2013- Mauritania
c2013- Niger
c2013- Nigeria
2014 Democratic Republic of the Congo
2014- Iraq
2014- Syria
2015 Democratic Republic of the Congo
c2015- Cameroon
2016 Democratic Republic of the Congo
2017- Saudi Arabia
c2017 Tunisia
2019- Philippines

Since its earliest days, but especially since World War II, this list suggests, U.S. imperialists have looked well beyond their hemisphere. This has not been an abandonment of the Monroe Doctrine so much as an expansion of it. The history of the Monroe Doctrine in practice, rather than in its words or in the myths that have been created around it, is one of opposing, supporting, and ultimately seeking to supersede the British empire, as well as the Spanish and other empires. Through that process, the Monroe Doctrine has provided a propaganda model, a justification for not only U.S. imperialism, but also the imperialism of others, and for a new form of imperialism in which traditional conquest is replaced by quieter influence and control. The U.S. government began by actively promoting the concept of a Monroe Doctrine to others, in particular to the Japanese.

After the U.S. had forced its way into Japan, it groomed Japan as a junior partner in imperialism, worthy of its own "Monroe Doctrine for Asia." Lacking a single god or a god of conquest, the Japanese invented a divine emperor, borrowing heavily from Christian tradition. They dressed and dined like Americans and sent their students to study in the United States. The Japanese were often referred to in the United States as the "Yankees of the Far East." In 1872 the U.S. military began training the Japanese in how to conquer other nations, with an eye on Taiwan. Charles LeGendre, a U.S. general training the Japanese in the ways of war, proposed that they adopt a Monroe Doctrine for Asia, that is a policy of dominating Asia in the way that the United States dominated, or at least claimed to dominate, its hemisphere. Japan established a Bureau of Savage Affairs and invented new words like koronii (colony). (The U.S. government would not cease referring to its colonies of the Philippines, Puerto Rico, Guam, etc., with the word "colony" until 1914.)[197] Talk in Japan began to focus on the responsibility of the Japanese to civilize the savages. In 1873, Japan invaded Taiwan with U.S. military advisors. Korea was next.

Korea and Japan had known peace for centuries. When the Japanese arrived with U.S. ships, wearing U.S. clothing, talking about their divine emperor, and proposing a treaty of "friendship," the Koreans, like Native Americans before them, thought their conquerors had lost their minds, and told them to get lost, knowing that China was there at Korea's back. But the Japanese talked China into allowing Korea to sign the treaty, without explaining to either the Chinese or Koreans what the treaty meant in its English language version.

In 1894 Japan declared war on China, a war in which U.S. weapons, on the Japanese side, carried the day. China gave up Taiwan and the Liaodong Peninsula, paid a large indemnity, declared Korea independent, and gave Japan the same commercial rights in China that the U.S. and European nations had. Japan was triumphant, until China persuaded Russia, France, and Germany to oppose Japanese ownership of Liaodong. Japan gave it up and Russia grabbed it. Japan felt betrayed by white Christians, and not for the last time.

In 1904, Theodore Roosevelt was very pleased with a Japanese surprise attack on Russian ships. As the Japanese again waged war on Asia as honorary Aryans, Roosevelt secretly and unconstitutionally cut deals with them, approving a Monroe Doctrine for Japan in Asia. In the 1930s, Japan offered to open up trade to the United States in its imperial sphere if the United States would do the same for Japan in Latin America. The U.S. government said no.[198]

In the 20th century the U.S. and Japan grew apart. By the 1930s, they were trading insults and steps in an arms race. U.S. ambition had grown to include Asia within its vision of its own Monroe Doctrine. There would be no room for a Japanese sphere of domination. There would be no room anywhere on Earth for an acceptable sphere of domination for anyone other than the United States. As noted above, Theodore Roosevelt spoke of the Monroe Doctrine in global terms, and Woodrow Wilson wished for "the doctrine of President Monroe" to be the "doctrine of the world." In campaigning for the League of Nations, Wilson urged that the United States "accept what is offered to us, the leadership of the world."[199] The League of Nations was rejected by the United States Senate, not simply because people wanted to "isolate" themselves from the world or even because they were angry at the catastrophe of World War I; and not only because Wilson alienated all kinds of people with his racism, his attacks on labor, and his anti-communist witch hunts; and certainly not because Wilson was a saintly altruist trapped in a world of selfish hillbillies; but also because the League of Nations would have fallen short of handing the United States the leadership of the world, would in fact have made the United States one nation among others.

But Wilson believed that the United States could dominate through a structure as fair as the League of Nations, because he believed that commercial and financial power were growing in importance relative to the power of military conquest. According to Neil Smith, "Wilson's genius was to have figured out that the future of US power in the world was not dependent, as European power had been (and arguably as all other power in world history had been), on direct territorial control. It could, rather, be organized through the market. This is not to say that territorial control was never important—Wilson fought over territorial arrangements at Paris as hard as anyone, and in other contexts he sent his fair share of marines to Latin America—but he did perceive that the most central achievement in Paris did not concern any particular territory but rather the creation of a political system that would absorb territorial conflicts while allowing economic business to proceed as usual. This was the subtext to his popular slogan that he wanted to 'make the world safe for democracy.'"[200] In other words, there are not two irreconcilable Woodrow Wilsons, the KKK-promoting imperialist propagandist and destroyer of civil liberties on the one hand, and the advocate of open and accountable human brotherhood and equality on the other, because what Wilson wanted on the international stage was not only white supremacy but U.S. supremacy. In the years that followed, U.S. foreign policy elites would increasingly agree.

Stephen Wertheim's 2020 book, *Tomorrow, The World,* examines a shift in elite U.S. foreign-policy thinking that took place in mid-1940. Why in that moment, a year and a half before the Japanese attacks on the Philippines, Hawaii, and other outposts, did it become popular in foreign-policy circles to advocate for U.S. military domination of the globe?[201]

In school text book mythology, the United States was full of revoltingly backward creatures called isolationists at the time of World War I and right up through December 1941, after which the rational adult internationalists took command (or we'd all be speaking German). In fact, the term "isolationist" wasn't cooked up until the mid-1930s and then only as a misleading insult to be applied to people who wished for the U.S. government to engage with the world in any number of ways from treaties to trade that didn't include militarism. Anti-isolationism was and is a means of ridiculously pretending that "doing something" means waging war, supporting NATO, and promoting the "responsibility to protect," while anything else means "doing nothing."

There were distinctions in the 1920s between those who favored the League of Nations and World Court and those who didn't. But neither group favored coating the planet with U.S. military bases, or extending even the most vicious conception of the Monroe Doctrine to the other hemisphere, or replacing the League of Nations with an institution that would falsely appear to establish global governance while actually facilitating U.S. domination. Pre-1940 internationalists were, in fact, imperfect U.S. nationalists. They, as Wertheim writes, "had the capacity to see the United States as a potential aggressor requiring restraint." Some, indeed, didn't need the word "potential" there.

What changed? There was the rise of fascism and communism. There was the notion that the League of Nations had failed. There was the serious failure of disarmament efforts. There was the belief that whatever came out of WWII would be dramatically different. In September 1939, the Council on Foreign Relations began making plans to shape the post-war (so-called but involving unending war) world. The Franklin Roosevelt White House into 1940 was planning for a post-war world that held a balance of power with the Nazis. Ideas of disarmament, at least for others, were still very much a part of the thinking. "Weapons dealer to the world" was not a title that it was ever suggested that the United States strive for.

Wertheim sees a turning point in the German conquest of France. Change came swiftly in May-June, 1940. Congress funded the creation of the world's biggest navy and instituted a draft. Contrary to popular mythology, and propaganda pushed by President Roosevelt, nobody feared a Nazi invasion of the Americas. Nor was the United States dragged kicking and screaming into its moral responsibility to wage global permawar by the atrocious domestic policies of the Nazis or any mission to rescue potential victims from Nazi genocide. Rather, U.S. foreign policy elites feared the impact on global trade and relations of a world containing a Nazi power. Roosevelt began talking about a world in which the United States dominated only a single hemisphere as "imprisonment."

The United States needed to dominate the globe in order to exist in the sort of global order it wanted. And the only global order it wanted was one it dominated. Did U.S. planners become aware of this need as they watched events in Europe? Or did they become aware of its possibility as they watched the U.S. government build weapons and the U.S. president acquire new imperial bases? Probably some of each. Wertheim is right to call our attention to the fact that U.S. officials didn't talk about militarily dominating the whole globe prior to 1940, but was there ever a time they talked about dominating anything less than what they had the weapons and troops to handle? Certainly the voices had not all been monolithic, and there was always an anti-imperialist tradition, but did the United States ever give much back to those it had dispossessed until after WWII when airplanes and radios developed a new sort of empire (and some colonies were made states but others more or less liberated)?

The U.S. government and its advisers didn't just discover that they could rule the world and that they needed to rule the world, but also that — in the words of General George V. Strong, chief of the Army's War Plans Division — Germany had demonstrated the "tremendous advantage of the offense over the defense." The proper defensive war was an aggressive war, and an acceptable goal of that was what Henry Luce called living space and Hitler called Lebensraum. U.S. elites came to believe that only through war could they engage in proper trade and relations. One can treat this as a rational observation based on the growth of fascism, although some of the same people making the observation had fascistic tendencies. The problem with Germany seems to have existed for these people only once Germany had invaded other nations that were not Russia, and there is little doubt that had the United States lived sustainably, locally, egalitarianly, contentedly, and with respect for all humanity, it could not have observed a need for permawar in the world around it — much less gone on observing it for decades thereafter.

In early 1941, a U.S. political scientist named Harold Vinacke asked, "When the United States has its thousands of airplanes, its mass army, properly mechanized, and its two-ocean navy, what are they to be used for?" Officials have been asking the same right up through Madeline Albright and Donald Trump, with the answer generally being found to be as self-evident as other patriotic "truths."

By summertime 1941, Roosevelt and Churchill had announced the future organization of the world in the Atlantic Charter.

If hypocrisy is the compliment that vice pays to virtue, there remained some virtue in U.S. society and its conception of foreign policy at the time of WWII, because a major focus of post-war planners was how to sell global domination to the U.S. public (and incidentally the world, and perhaps most importantly themselves) as being something other than what it was. The answer, of course, was the United Nations (along with the World Bank, etc.). Undersecretary of State Sumner Welles described the design of the United Nations thus: "what we required was a sop for the smaller states: some organization in which they could be represented and made to feel themselves participants." In Roosevelt's words before the creation of the U.N., all nations but four, in a future global organization, would merely "blow off steam."

Roosevelt also proposed that the existence of such a phony organization would allow it to declare war instead of the U.S. Congress, meaning that a U.S. president would be able to launch wars at will — something like what we've seen for the past several decades, with NATO occasionally having filled in for a malfunctioning United Nations.

Roosevelt believed that the United States signed up for global policeman when it defeated Hitler. Neither Roosevelt nor Wertheim mentions that the Soviet Union did 80% of defeating Hitler, after having done about 0% of creating him. Nor has it been popular to this day to question how a global policeman with the duty to protect democracy can appoint himself to office against the will of much of the world. Clearly, taking the Monroe Doctrine global is to grab a privilege (even if you claim it's a responsibility) that you are simultaneously denying to anyone else.

The Monroe Doctrine, or the speech it was part of, committed the United States to staying out of Europe. The United States did not stay out of Europe. It took part in World War I, World War II, and wars in the former Yugoslavia and now in Ukraine. It facilitated color revolutions. It loaded the place up with U.S.-made weapons, currently maintaining U.S. nuclear weapons in six European countries. It left forces behind after World War II to sabotage European democracies. And it created a military alliance called NATO, that it claimed not to dominate, but clearly dominated, and on which it bestowed a Monroe Doctrine. The Warsaw Pact also saw itself as guardian of a Monroe Doctrine, a Russian sphere of nearby domination for the sake of self-protection from powerful imperial forces. NATO, and to a lesser extent other alliances, such as SEATO, have used Monroe Doctrine thinking to expand militarism and U.S. influence. From the birth of the Monroe Doctrine, the threats addressed have typically been exaggerated or wholly fabricated. So, it is not shocking that the elimination of the Warsaw Pact led not to the dismantling of NATO but to its expansion.

The U.S. government believes quite rightly that it would be outrageous for any other nation to impose a Monroe Doctrine on any part of the globe, yet it insists on its right to impose one on the entire globe. Russia believes that Eastern Europe, and China believes that the South China Sea, is in its neighborhood, and that the U.S. government has no business there. The U.S. government believes that those locations are on its planet, where it has a right to everywhere. Neither Russia nor China should be imposing its will on neighboring nations, but the last voice capable of effectively making that point is that of the U.S. government.

Blowback from the global pursuit of a Monroe Doctrine has of course included anti-U.S. sentiment and violence. In addition, occasionally the reliance on coups abroad has contributed to the risk of one in Washington, D.C. The old joke is to ask "Why is there never a coup in Washington?" and to answer "Because it has no U.S. embassy." But we know of multiple coup plots against Franklin Roosevelt: the one undone by Smedley Butler, and one recounted in the autobiography of Cornelius Vanderbilt IV who said he had exposed a coup plot to Eleanor Roosevelt and thereby to her husband, and thereby successfully put a stop to it. Apparently a separate and third coup plot against FDR was that in 1940 of Father Coughlin's pro-Nazi Christian Front militia, aka the Brooklyn Boys.[202] A fourth coup plot or collections of coup efforts is found in the 1940s federal indictment and re-indictment for sedition of some 30 men and women for conspiring to create a Nazi government in the United States, and the trial that opened in Washington, D.C., on April 17th, 1944. This included people like George Deatherage, who had plotted fascist violence, and people tied to Nazi agent George Viereck and members of Congress who had spread Nazi propaganda in the United States. Openly pro-Nazi defendants were permitted, with assistance by Congress Members, to bully the court into a mistrial.[203]

Then there was January 6, 2021, when people intent on keeping Donald Trump as president despite an election loss stormed the U.S. Capitol. At the very least, it seems to me that the U.S. government and corporate media's contempt for democratic government abroad does little to increase respect for it within the United States.

Perhaps the influence also blows back outward. On January 8, 2023, in Brasilia, a Trumpy2021-like coup attempt (or coup-like demonstration) was staged by supporters of former president and defeated candidate for reelection Jair Messias Bolsonaro, who was hiding out from Brazilian criminal prosecution in the United States.

7. What Should Be Done?

The trend of Latin American elections toward independence-minded presidents and the success in resisting and reversing coups are highly encouraging, but far from sufficient. Imagine if the United States had just elected a president on a platform of independence from Ecuadorean influence, but Ecuador not only had that ludicrous military base in Miami, Florida, but also had numerous Ecuadorean military bases across the United States, and those bases so long established as to be hardly noticed, thought about, questioned, or challenged.

To some significant extent, the U.S. government doesn't need what FDR called "our sonofabitch" running each Latin American country anymore. It has those bases, those weapons customers, those U.S.-trained troops, U.S.-educated elites, corporate trade agreements that overrule constitutions, and the financial powers of debt, aid, and sanctions. The struggle to impose the Monroe Doctrine by one means or another is alive and well. In 2022, the *Wall Street Journal* insisted that the Earth's climate (how's that for a new excuse?) would require that corporations, and not the nations of Bolivia, Chile, and Argentina, control lithium.[204] How did our lithium get under their ground?

Coups are not forgotten. In 2022, when Colombia elected its first-ever left-leaning president, U.S. President Biden's top Latin American advisor, Western Hemisphere director for the National Security Council Juan Sebastián González, went on a Columbian media outlet. Speaking in Spanish, he declared that "40 years ago, the United States would have done everything possible to prevent the election of Gustavo Petro, and once in power it would have done almost everything possible to sabotage his government."[205] González said those policies were things of the past, and that the U.S. now has no imperial agenda. But of course that second point doesn't follow from the first one, even if the first one were true.

However, this is a moment in which the U.S. government is at least somewhat distracted by Ukraine and willing to purchase Venezuelan oil if it believes that contributes to hurting Russia. And it is a moment of tremendous accomplishment and aspiration in Latin America.

In 2021, on the 238th anniversary of Simón Bolívar's birth, Mexican President Andrés Manuel López Obrador ("AMLO") gave a speech in which he proposed to recreate Bolívar's "project of unity among the peoples of Latin America and the Caribbean."[206] AMLO said that "the struggle for the integrity of the peoples of our America continues to be a beautiful ideal. It has not been easy to make that beautiful purpose a reality. Its main obstacles have been the conservative movement of the nations of America, the ruptures in the ranks of the liberal movement, and the dominance of the United States in the continent. Let us not forget that almost at the same time that our countries became independent from Spain and other European nations, the new metropolis of hegemonic domination began to emerge on this continent."

AMLO provides a history of the Monroe Doctrine:

> *"During the difficult period of the wars of independence, generally inaugurated around 1810, American rulers, with entirely pragmatic optics, followed events with stealthy interest. The United States maneuvered at different times according to a unilateral game: extreme caution at the beginning, so as not to irritate Spain, Great Britain, the Holy Alliance, without hindering decolonization, which at times seemed doubtful; However, around 1822, Washington began the rapid recognition of the independence achieved in order to block the path to extracontinental interventionism, and in 1823, finally, a defined policy. In October, Jefferson, progenitor of the Declaration of Independence and by then converted into a kind of oracle, responded by letter to a query made to him by President Monroe*

on the matter. In a significant paragraph, Jefferson says: "Our first and fundamental maxim should be never to mix in the imbroglios of Europe. The second, never allow Europe to meddle in the affairs of this side of the Atlantic." In December, Monroe delivered the famous speech outlining the doctrine that bears his name. The slogan of "America for the Americans" ended up disintegrating the peoples of our continent and destroying what was built, the material, by Bolívar. Throughout almost the entire 19th century it suffered from constant occupations, landings, annexations and it cost us the loss of half of our territory, with the great blow of 1848. This territorial and warlike expansion of the United States was consecrated when Cuba, the last stronghold of Spain in America, fell in 1898, with the suspicious sinking of the battleship Maine in Havana, which gave rise to the Platt Amendment and the occupation of Guantanamo; that is to say, by then the United States had finished defining its physical-vital space in all of America. Since that time, Washington has never stopped conducting overt or covert operations against the independent countries south of the Rio Grande.

"The influence of U.S. foreign policy is predominant in America. There is only one special case, that of Cuba, the country that for more than half a century has asserted its independence by politically confronting the United States. We may or may not agree with the Cuban Revolution and its government, but having resisted 62 years without submission is quite a feat. My words may provoke anger in some or many, but as the song by René Pérez Joglar from Calle 13 says: "I always say what I think". Consequently, I believe that, for their fight in defense of the sovereignty of their country, the people of Cuba deserve the award of dignity and that island should be considered the new Numancia for its example of resistance, and I think that for the same reason it should be declared a World Heritage Site. But I also maintain that it is time for a new coexistence among

all the countries of the Americas, because the model imposed more than two centuries ago is exhausted, it has no future or way out, it no longer benefits anyone."

AMLO proposes a way out:

"We must put aside the dilemma of joining the United States or opposing it defensively. It is time to express and explore another option: to dialogue with the U.S. rulers and convince and persuade them that a new relationship between the countries of the Americas is possible. I believe that currently there are unbeatable conditions to achieve this purpose of respecting each other and walking together without leaving anyone behind. In this effort, our experience of economic integration with respect to our sovereignty, which we have put into practice in the conception and application of the economic and commercial agreement with the United States and Canada, may help. Obviously, it is no small thing to have a nation like the United States as a neighbor. Our closeness forces us to seek agreements and it would be a serious mistake to kick Samson, but at the same time we have powerful reasons to assert our sovereignty and demonstrate with arguments, without braggadocio, that we are not a protectorate, a colony, or its back yard. In addition, with the passage of time, little by little a favorable circumstance for our country has been accepted: the excessive growth of China has strengthened the opinion in the United States that we should be seen as allies and not as distant neighbors.

"The integration process has been taking place since 1994, when the first treaty was signed, which is still incomplete, because it did not address the labor issue, like the one now, it allowed the installation of auto parts plants in the automotive sector and other branches and productive chains have been created that make us mutually indispensable. It can be said that even the U.S. military industry

depends on auto parts that are manufactured in Mexico. I do not say this with pride but to underline the existing interdependence. But speaking of this matter, as I commented to President Biden, we prefer economic integration with a sovereign dimension with the United States and Canada, in order to recover what we lost with respect to production and trade with China, than continue to weaken ourselves as a region and having a scenario plagued by war tensions in the Pacific. To put it in other words, it is in our interest for the United States to be strong economically and not just militarily. Achieving this balance and not the hegemony of any country is the most responsible and most convenient way to maintain peace for the good of future generations and of humanity."

AMLO warns against continuing with current trends:

"First of all we must be realistic and accept, as I stated in the speech I gave at the White House in July of last year, that while China commands 12.2 percent of the world export and services market, the United States only does so in 9.5 percent; And this gap dates back just 30 years, since in 1990 China's share was 1.3 percent and the United States' was 12.4 percent. Imagine if this trend of the last three decades continued, and there is nothing legally or legitimately to stop it, in another 30 years, by 2051, China would command 64.8 percent of the world market and the United States between 4 and 4. 10 percent; which, I insist, in addition to an unacceptable disproportion in the economic field, would keep alive the temptation to bet on resolving this disparity with the use of force, which would put us all in danger."

AMLO urges opening the U.S. border to immigrants:

"Why not study the demand for labor and, in an orderly manner, open the migratory flow? And within the framework of this new

joint development plan, investment policy, labor, environmental protection and other issues of mutual interest to our nations must be considered. It is obvious that this must imply cooperation for the development and well-being of all the peoples of Latin America and the Caribbean. The politics of the last two centuries, characterized by invasions to install or remove rulers at the whim of the superpower, is already unacceptable; Let's say goodbye to impositions, interference, sanctions, exclusions, and blockades. Instead, let us apply the principles of non-intervention, self-determination of peoples and the peaceful settlement of disputes. Let's start a relationship in our continent under the premise of George Washington, according to which, 'nations should not take advantage of the misfortune of other peoples.'"

AMLO proposes a European Union for Latin America:

"I am aware that this is a complex issue that requires a new political and economic vision: the proposal is neither more nor less than building something similar to the European Union, but attached to our history, our reality and our identities. In this spirit, the replacement of the OAS by a truly autonomous body should not be ruled out, not a lackey for anyone, but a mediator at the request and acceptance of the parties in conflict, in matters of human rights and democracy. It is a great task for good diplomats and politicians like those that, fortunately, exist in all the countries of our continent. What is proposed here may seem like a utopia; however, it should be considered that without the horizon of ideals you will not get anywhere and that, consequently, it is worth trying. Let's keep Bolivar's dream alive."

Like any politician, AMLO speaks better than he acts, and even when speaking proposes ideas merely for consideration rather than insisting that they be acted upon. But a speech is an act, and one that can inspire others, as this one has. And AMLO has taken other actions. He has worked to undo U.S. immigration policies through the Inter-American Commission on Human Rights.[207] He has led a boycott of a Summit of the Americas from which the Biden Administration sought to exclude those nations defying the United States' bidding (Nicaragua, Venezuela, and Cuba). In 2022, at the Summit of the Americas hosted by the United States, only 23 of 35 nations sent representatives. The United States had excluded three nations, while several others boycotted, including Mexico, Bolivia, Honduras, Guatemala, El Salvador, and Antigua and Barbuda. Also in 2022, Nicaragua completed the process of withdrawing from the OAS.

Of course, the U.S. government always claims it is excluding or punishing or seeking to overthrow nations because they are dictatorships, not because they are defying U.S. interests. But, as I documented in my 2020 book *20 Dictators Currently Supported by the United States*, of the world's 50 most oppressive governments at that time, by the U.S. government's own understanding, the United States militarily supported 48 of them, allowing (or even funding) weapons sales to 41 of them, providing military training to 44 of them, and providing funding to the militaries of 33 of them.

AMLO also rejected a proposal from then-U.S. President Trump for a joint war against drug dealers, proposing in the process the abolition of war:[208]

> *"The worst that could be, the worst thing we could see, would be war. Those who have read about war, or those who have suffered from a war, know what war means. War is the opposite of politics. I have always said that politics was invented to avoid war. War is synonymous with irrationality. War is irrational. We are for peace. Peace is a principle of this new government. Authoritarians have no place in this government that I represent. It should be written out*

100 times as punishment: we declared war and it did not work. That is not an option. That strategy failed. We will not be a part of that. . . . Killing is not intelligence, which requires more than brute force."

The changing of the times can also be seen in the trajectory from Lima to Puebla.[209] In 2017, Canada, as Monroe-Doctrine-Junior-Partner (never mind if Monroe supported taking over Canada) took the lead in organizing the Lima Group, an organization of American nations intent on overthrowing the government of Venezuela. Members included Brazil, Canada, Chile, Colombia, Costa Rica, Ecuador, El Salvador, Guatemala, Haiti, Honduras, Paraguay, Peru, and Venezuela (the pretend Venezuela governed in his own mind by Juan Guaidó). But nations have been dropping out to the point that it's not clear anything is left. Meanwhile, in 2019, the Puebla Group of Members of Parliament from Latin American nations was formed. In 2022, it issued a statement:[210]

"Latin America and the Caribbean need to relaunch a financial architecture, adapted to their needs and without impositions, which threaten the sovereignty of our peoples and focus their gaze on the creation of a single Latin American currency. The Puebla Group confirms that drug trafficking has become a transnational and global problem. The main consuming countries must assume their responsibility in seeking a different solution to the problem. For this reason, we propose a Latin American alliance to find a solution based on the deregulation of drug prohibition, and to provide social and health treatment, and not exclusively criminal, to addiction and consumption.

"The Puebla Group must turn its Manifesto, launched in February 2021, into a series of concrete initiatives that have an impact on the well-being of Latin American and Caribbean people. To this end, a Solidarity Development Model was proposed last December whose

articulating axes are i) the search for equality as a central value of development and the reduction of global asymmetries ii) the search for value iii) a new economic policy, diversified and based on the incorporation of knowledge iv) the ecological transition v) a new democratic institutional framework and, vi) regional integration. . . .

"The region continues to observe criminal proceedings, trials with a political content and the legal war that evokes the fight against corruption as a justification, disguised as legality, to suppress progressive leadership from the political game, as has occurred against Cristina Fernández, Rafael Correa, Carlos Caicedo, Luis Inacio da Silva, Evo Morales, and Marco Enríquez-Ominami, among others. Thus, there are daily suspensions of rights and strategic uses of legal mechanisms to pursue popular political projects and take unfair retaliation against the opposition or political opponents. We highlight the efforts of the Latin American Council for Justice and Democracy (CLAJUD) to make lawfare visible and work tirelessly for Latin American sovereignty and respect for human rights.

"We see with genuine hope the 'total peace' in Colombia that ends the war that, for decades, has hindered the possibilities of full development and social justice. We support this approach that attacks the objective and social causes of violence and, as happened with the Havana Agreements, confirms that the only path to that long-awaited peace is negotiation and concertation, including all the actors.

"We need more integration and political dialogue. With the new panorama in Brazil, the way is cleared for its return to the Community of Latin American and Caribbean States (CELAC) and for the reactivation of the Union of South American Nations (UNASUR).

"Both spaces were weakened when the neoliberal governments were in the majority. However, their permanence cannot depend on changes in government, since they are essential spaces for regional agreement. Latin America needs to give new meaning to UNASUR and strengthen CELAC and, incidentally, to relaunch the convergence project that presupposes the articulation of other regional initiatives."

Bolivian President Evo Morales had declared in 2018 that, "the South American Parliament [UNASUR] is the center of integration and the symbol of the liberation of Latin America. The integration of all of Latin America is a path without return." In 2022, the Sao Paulo Forum organization of leftist parties called for the reconstitution of UNASUR: "We are in a historic moment for resuming and deepening the transformations in the economic and geopolitical fields that have occurred since the beginning of the century, and for accelerating the transition to a democratic multipolar world, one based on new international relations of cooperation and solidarity."[211] At the same time, representatives of Indigenous peoples from 16 countries met in Guatemala to organize a campaign for decolonization.[212]

This is all very encouraging. But for those of us in the United States, what should we be demanding of the U.S. government? An announcement that the Monroe Doctrine is dead? We've had those for about 100 years! We've been living in the supposed twilight of the Monroe Doctrine for as long as anyone now alive has been alive. What we need is the actual elimination of the structures of Monroe Doctrinism, and not because their time has passed, but because there never was a time when it was justifiable to impose one people's will on another. The Monroe Doctrine never had to be. History could have been worse, but it also could have been better.

Latin America never needed U.S. military bases, and they should all be shut down right now. Latin America would always have been better off without U.S. militarism (or anyone else's militarism) and should be liberated from the disease immediately. No more weapons sales. No more weapons gifts. No more military training or funding. No more U.S. militarized training of Latin American police or prison guards. No more exporting south the disastrous project of mass incarceration.[213] (A bill in Congress like the Berta Caceres Act that would cut off U.S. funding for military and police in Honduras as long as the latter are engaged in human rights abuses should be expanded to all of Latin America and the rest of the world, and made permanent without conditions; aid should take the form of financial relief, not armed troops.) No more war on drugs, abroad or at home. No more use of a war on drugs on behalf of militarism. No more ignoring the poor quality of life or the poor quality of healthcare that create and sustain drug abuse. No more environmentally and humanly destructive trade agreements. No more celebration of economic "growth" for its own sake. No more competition with China or anyone else, commercial or martial. No more debt. (Cancel it!) No more aid with strings attached. No more collective punishment through sanctions. No more border walls or senseless impediments to free movement. No more second-class citizenship. No more diversion of resources away from environmental and human crises into updated versions of the archaic practice of conquest. Latin America never needed U.S. colonialism. Puerto Rico, and all U.S. territories, should be permitted to choose independence or statehood, and along with either choice, reparations.

A major step in this direction could be taken by the U.S. government through the simple abolition of one little rhetorical practice: hypocrisy. You want to be part of a "rules-based order"? Then join one! There is one out there waiting for you, and Latin America is leading it.

Of the United Nations' 18 major human rights treaties, the United States is party to 5, fewer than any other nation on earth, except Bhutan (4), and tied with Malaysia, Myanmar, and South Sudan, a country torn by warfare since its creation in 2011. The United States is the only nation on

Earth that has not ratified the Convention on the Rights of the Child. It is by many measures a top destroyer of the natural environment, yet has been a leader in sabotaging climate protection negotiations for decades and has never ratified the UN Framework Convention on Climate Control (UNFCCC) and the Kyoto Protocol. The U.S. government has never ratified the Comprehensive Test Ban Treaty and withdrew from the Anti-Ballistic Missile (ABM) Treaty in 2001. It has never signed the Mine Ban Treaty or the Convention on Cluster Munitions.

The United States leads opposition to democratization of the United Nations and easily holds the record for use of the veto in the Security Council during the past 50 years, having vetoed U.N. condemnation of South African apartheid, Israel's wars and occupations, chemical and biological weapons, nuclear weapons proliferation and first use and use against non-nuclear nations, U.S. wars in Nicaragua and Grenada and Panama, the U.S. embargo on Cuba, Rwandan genocide, the deployment of weapons in outer space, etc.

Contrary to popular opinion, the United States is not a leading provider of aid to the suffering of the world, not as a percentage of gross national income or per capita or even as an absolute number of dollars. Unlike other countries, the United States counts as 40 percent of its so-called aid, weapons for foreign militaries. Its aid as a whole is directed around its military goals, and its immigration policies have long been shaped around skin color, and lately around religion, not around human need — except perhaps inversely, focusing on locking up and building walls to punish the most desperate.[214]

The laws we need mostly don't require imagining, or even enacting, just complying with. Since 1945, all parties to the UN Charter have been compelled to "settle their international disputes by peaceful means in such a manner that international peace and security, and justice, are not endangered," and to "refrain in their international relations from the threat or use of force against the territorial integrity or political independence of any state," albeit with loopholes added for UN-authorized wars and wars of "self-defense," (but never for the threatening of war) — loopholes that do not apply to any recent wars, but loopholes the existence of which create in many minds the vague idea that wars are legal. The requirement of peace and ban on war has been elaborated over the years in various UN resolutions, such as Resolutions 2625 and 3314. The parties to the Charter would end war were they to comply with it.

Since 1949, all parties to NATO, have agreed to a restatement of the ban on threatening or using force found in the UN Charter, even while agreeing to prepare for wars and to join in the defensive wars waged by other members of NATO. The vast majority of the Earth's weapons dealing and military spending, and a huge portion of its war making, is done by NATO members.

Since 1949, parties to the Fourth Geneva Convention have been forbidden to engage in any violence toward individuals not actively engaged in war, and banned from all use of "[c]ollective penalties and likewise all measures of intimidation or of terrorism," while meanwhile the vast majority of those killed in wars have been non-combatants, and deadly sanctions are not given a second thought. All the big war makers are party to the Geneva Conventions.

Since 1951, parties to the OAS Charter have agreed that "No State or group of States has the right to intervene, directly or indirectly, for any reason whatever, in the internal or external affairs of any other State." If the U.S. government thought for an instant that a treaty was the supreme law of the land, as the U.S. Constitution makes it, rather than a means of tricking Native Americans and others, this would have been understood as the criminalizing of the Monroe Doctrine.

The United States does not need to "reverse course and lead the world" as the common demand would have it on most topics where the United States is behaving destructively. The United States needs, on the contrary, to join the world and try to catch up with Latin America which has taken the lead on creating a better world. Two continents dominate the membership of the International Criminal Court and strive most seriously to uphold international law: Europe and the Americas south of Texas. Latin America leads the way in membership in the Treaty on the Prohibition of Nuclear Weapons. Virtually all of Latin America is part of a nuclear weapons free zone, out ahead of any other continent, apart from Australia.

Latin American nations support the international rule of law even when they're domestic disasters. They join and uphold treaties as well or better than anywhere else on Earth. They have no nuclear, chemical, or biological weapons -- despite having U.S. military bases. Only Brazil exports weapons and the amount is relatively tiny. Since 2014, the over 30 member states of the Community of Latin American and Caribbean States (CELAC) have been bound by this Declaration of a Zone of Peace:

> *"1. Latin America and the Caribbean as a Zone of Peace based on respect for the principles and rules of International Law, including the international instruments to which Member States are a party to, the Principles and Purposes of the United Nations Charter;*
> *"2. Our permanent commitment to solve disputes through peaceful means with the aim of uprooting forever threat or use of force in our region;*
> *"3. The commitment of the States of the region with their strict obligation not to intervene, directly or indirectly, in the internal affairs of any other State and observe the principles of national sovereignty, equal rights and self-determination of peoples;*
> *"4. The commitment of the peoples of Latin American and Caribbean to foster cooperation and friendly relations among themselves*

and with other nations irrespective of differences in their political, economic, and social systems or development levels; to practice tolerance and live together in peace with one another as good neighbors;

"5. The commitment of the Latin American and Caribbean States to fully respect for the inalienable right of every State to choose its political, economic, social, and cultural system, as an essential conditions to ensure peaceful coexistence among nations;

"6. The promotion in the region of a culture of peace based, inter alia, on the principles of the United Nations Declaration on a Culture of Peace;

"7. The commitment of the States in the region to guide themselves by this Declaration in their International behavior;

"8. The commitment of the States of the region to continue promoting nuclear disarmament as a priority objective and to contribute with general and complete disarmament, to foster the strengthening of confidence among nations."

It's one thing to say you oppose war. It's another entirely to be placed in a situation in which many would tell you that war is the only option and use a superior option instead. Leading the way in demonstrating this wiser course is Latin America. In 1931, Chileans overthrew a dictator nonviolently.[215] In 1933 and again in 1935, Cubans overthrew presidents using general strikes.[216] In 1944, three dictators, Maximiliano Hernandez Martinez (El Salvador), Jorge Ubico (Guatemala), and Carlos Arroyo del Río (Ecuador) were ousted as a result of nonviolent civilian insurrections.[217] In 1946, Haitians nonviolently overthrew a dictator.[218] (Perhaps World War II and "good neighborism" gave Latin America a bit of a respite from the "aid" of its northern neighbor.) In 1957, Colombians nonviolently overthrew a dictator.[219] In 1982 in Bolivia, people nonviolently prevented a military coup.[220] In 1983, Mothers of the Plaza de Mayo won democratic reform and the return of (some of) their "disappeared" family members through nonviolent action.[221] In 1984, Uruguayans ended a military government with a general strike.[222] In 1987, the people of Argentina nonviolently prevented a military coup.[223] In 1988, Chileans nonviolently overthrew the Pinochet regime.[224] In 1992, Brazilians nonviolently drove out a corrupt president.[225] In 2000, Peruvians nonviolently overthrew the dictator Alberto Fujimori.[226] In 2005, Ecuadorians nonviolently ousted a corrupt president.[227] In Ecuador, a community has for years used strategic nonviolent action and communication to turn back an armed takeover of land by a mining company.[228] In 2015, Guatemalans compelled a corrupt president to resign.[229] In Colombia, a community has claimed its land and largely removed itself from war.[230] Another community in Mexico has been doing the same.[231] In Canada, in recent years, indigenous people have used nonviolent action to prevent the armed installation of pipelines on their lands.[232] The pink tide election results in recent years in Latin America are also the result of a great deal of nonviolent activism.

Latin America offers numerous innovative models to learn from and develop, including many indigenous societies living sustainably and peacefully, including the Zapatistas using largely and increasingly nonviolent activism to advance democratic and socialist ends, and including the example of Costa Rica abolishing its military, placing that military in a museum where it belongs, and being the better off for it.[233]

Latin America also offers models for something that is badly needed for the Monroe Doctrine: a truth and reconciliation commission. A truth commission was held in Argentina, with a report released in 1984 on the "disappearing" of people between 1976 and 1983. Truth commissions released reports in Chile in 1991 and El Salvador in 1993. These all preceded the well-known truth and reconciliation commission in South Africa, and others have followed. There is a great deal yet to be done in Latin America, and many are hard at work.[234] A truth commission and criminal prosecutions of torture have uncovered a lot of truth in Guatemala, with much left to be revealed.[235]

In Chile people are working, thus far without success, to create a new progressive constitution, to replace that of the Pinochet era. Some are attempting to make a ban on war part of the new Chilean constitution.[236] But few constitutions in Latin America are not more advanced than that of the United States. In Ecuador the constitution is committed to peaceful behavior by Ecuador and a ban on militarism by anyone else in Ecuador:

> *"Ecuador is a territory of peace. The establishment of foreign military bases or foreign facilities for military purposes shall not be allowed. It is forbidden to transfer national military bases to foreign armed or security forces. . . . It promotes peace and universal disarmament; it condemns the development and use of weapons of mass destruction and the imposition of bases or facilities for military purposes by certain States on the territory of others."*

Other constitutions that ban foreign military bases include those of Bolivia, Nicaragua, and Venezuela.

In Guyana today, a lawsuit seeks to prevent ExxonMobil from extracting huge quantities of climate-destroying oil. The lawsuit relies on the right to a sustainable environment that was established in Guyana's constitution.[237]

Latin American nations, despite Colombia's partnership with NATO (unaltered apparently by its new government), have not been eager to join in a U.S.- and NATO-backed war between Ukraine and Russia, or to condemn or financially sanction only one side of it. In March 2022, former Bolivian president Evo Morales said, "NATO is a danger to world peace, to security, so we are working on reaching agreements with social movements, not only in Latin America, but in all continents, to eliminate it. If nothing is done against NATO, it will become a permanent threat to humanity."[238] Of course, residents of nations closer to Russia than to the United States are more likely to concentrate on the imperialistic outrages of the Russian military, while it's difficult for someone from Latin America not to focus on U.S. imperialism. But both critiques are correct. The U.S. global Monroe Doctrine doesn't justify a Russian Monroe Doctrine in Europe. Human survival depends on moving beyond the idea of "a multipolar world" or warring tribes as the solution.

The task before the United States, where I live, is to end its Monroe Doctrine, and to end it not only in Latin America but globally, and to not only end it but to replace it with the positive actions of joining the world as a law-abiding member, upholding the rule of international law, and cooperating on nuclear disarmament, environmental protection, disease epidemics, homelessness, and poverty. The Monroe Doctrine was never a law, and laws now in place forbid it. There's nothing to be repealed or enacted. What's needed is simply the sort of decent behavior that U.S. politicians increasingly pretend they're already engaged in.

While we're abolishing the Monroe Doctrine, why not the very idea of doctrines and all existing doctrines as well?

In 2018, Karl Walling of the U.S. Naval War College wrote in a review of a book about presidential doctrines: "Syracusa and Warren do not say it, but the discerning reader can infer that the trajectory of American national security doctrines has resulted in an ironic consequence: that the United States, originally founded on the rule of law, with Washington's Farewell Address imploring Americans to respect international law, now reserves to itself the right to use force under any circumstances in which it considers its security threatened, regardless of whether it or its allies have been attacked, and with or without the support of allies and the legitimacy of international and multilateral support. They finished their book before the election of President Trump, but one might see his inchoate America First Doctrine as a continuation of this disturbing trend, including the acquiescence of Congress most of the time to presidential national security doctrines through vaguely worded authorizations to use military force (AUMFs), which presidents construe as license to fight almost any time, almost anywhere. Said James Madison in Federalist 10, 'Enlightened statesmen will not always be at the helm,' but now the United States and the world depend on the enlightenment of the president's national security advisers to prevent America First from degenerating into the sort of national narcissism that might make the United States the greatest rogue nation in history."[239]

The reference to President George Washington's Farewell Address is there because the book being reviewed included consideration of significant presidential ideas even if they had not become "doctrines," ideas like George Washington's warning against foreign wars, and Woodrow Wilson's support for the League of Nations (presented as an extension of the Monroe Doctrine's "counter intervention" policy). What if the thing that best summed up U.S. foreign policy during each era were made that era's doctrine? We'd certainly have more doctrines, including a bit more variety, though with a great deal of consistency remaining. We'd also have more honesty. Something like "Make sure to please U.S. weapons dealers and oil-selling dictatorships at all costs," despite never having been announced in a State of the Union address, would almost certainly enter into the rankings of most important doctrines.

But what if, instead, the most peaceful thing a president said were turned into his doctrine instead of this current practice of finding and enshrining his (or someday her) most belligerent utterance?

Even in the very same speech as the Monroe Doctrine, President James Monroe spoke in support of transparency in government and public decision making. He also said "It is by rendering justice to other nations that we may expect it from them." He made a case for the peaceful resolution of disputes with Britain, France, and Russia through negotiations and treaties.

In fact, the first supposed sentence of the Monroe Doctrine is actually not a complete sentence, but the continuation of a sentence putting it into the context of peaceful negotiations with Russia, the topic of the paragraph that the sentence concludes. And that paragraph is followed by discussion of peaceful negotiations with Russia and Spain. And that is followed by discussion of abolishing the slave trade. Any of this stuff would make a better doctrine than the existing Monroe Doctrine should we choose to make a change.

Scanning through presidents, off the top of my head, I can come up with some samples of what peaceful presidential doctrines might look like:

Peaceful Coolidge Doctrine:

"The foreign policy of America can best be described by one word — peace. . . . We covet no territory; we support no threatening military army; we harbor no hostile intent. We have pursued, are pursuing, and shall continue to pursue with untiring devotion the cause of peace. These ideas we have put into practical application. We have sought to promote peace not only by word, but by appropriate action."[240]

Peaceful Eisenhower Doctrine:

"Every gun that is made, every warship launched, every rocket fired signifies in the final sense, a theft from those who hunger and are not fed, those who are cold and are not clothed. This world in arms is not spending money alone. It is spending the sweat of its laborers, the genius of its scientists, the hopes of its children. This is not a way of life at all in any true sense. Under the clouds of war, it is humanity hanging on a cross of iron."

Peaceful Kennedy Doctrine:

"I speak of peace, therefore, as the necessary rational end of rational men. I realize that the pursuit of peace is not as dramatic as the pursuit of war–and frequently the words of the pursuer fall on deaf ears. But we have no more urgent task. Some say that it is useless to speak of world peace or world law or world disarmament–and that it will be useless until the leaders of the Soviet Union adopt a more enlightened attitude. I hope they do. I believe we can help them do it. But I also believe that we must reexamine our own attitude–as individuals and as a Nation–for our attitude is as essential as theirs. And every graduate of this school, every thoughtful citizen who despairs of war and wishes to bring peace, should begin by looking inward–by examining his own attitude toward the possibilities of peace, toward the Soviet Union, toward the course of the cold war and toward freedom and peace here at home."[241]

Peaceful Obama Doctrine:

"I don't want to just end the war, but I want to end the mindset that got us into war in the first place."

Peaceful Trump Doctrine:

"We've spent $4 trillion trying to topple various people that, frankly, if they were there and if we could have spent that $4 trillion in the United States to fix our roads, our bridges, and all of the other problems — our airports and all the other problems we have — we would have been a lot better off, I can tell you that right now. We have done a tremendous disservice not only to the Middle East — we've done a tremendous disservice to humanity. The people that have been killed, the people that have been wiped away — and for what? It's not like we had victory. It's a mess. The Middle East is totally destabilized, a total and complete mess. I wish we had the 4 trillion dollars or 5 trillion dollars. I wish it were spent right here in the United States on schools, hospitals, roads, airports, and everything else that are all falling apart!"

The Choice Is Ours

But wait, you say. That's the opposite of making the doctrines match the reality. Those statements don't sum up those eras. Those statements don't describe what the government did, or what the consensus was within the foreign policy blob. Those are just statements that one might wish had mattered more than they did.

But that's quite similar to what the current presidential doctrines are as well. They are statements that fail to sum up the foreign policy of an era, that pick out one element, and that highlight and promote that position, seeking to impose it on future generations through the stature of the name "Doctrine." Did Kennedy do more for war than peace in reality? I don't know. It's a tough call. But making a warlike position into his permanent soundbite "doctrine" is as inaccurate as was his own false depiction of what resolved the Cuban Missile Crisis (it was backing off and compromising, including withdrawing missiles from Turkey, but Kennedy told the media that bluster and threats had done the trick, and kept the missile withdrawals secret).[242]

The point is we have options when it comes to creating or accepting or taking seriously anybody's "doctrine" on anything, including Monroe's.

About the Author

David Swanson is an author, activist, journalist, and radio host. He is executive director of World BEYOND War and campaign coordinator for RootsAction.org. He blogs at DavidSwanson.org and WarIsACrime.org. He hosts Talk Nation Radio at TalkNationRadio.org. He is a Nobel Peace Prize Nominee, and was awarded the 2018 Peace Prize by the U.S. Peace Memorial Foundation.

Acknowledgements

All errors are mine alone.

Thank you to all the wonderful authors found in the end notes.

Thank you to Angela Marino, Brian Concannon, Linda Swanson, Roger Harris, and Tim Pluta.

Endnotes

1 James Monroe, "State of the Union Address," December 2, 1823, *Teaching American History*, https://teachingamericanhistory.org/document/state-of-the-union-address-33/.

2 "2022 National Defense Strategy of the United States of America," *United States Department of Defense,* October 27, 2022, https://media.defense.gov/2022/Oct/27/2003103845/-1/-1/1/2022-NATIONAL-DEFENSE-STRATEGY-NPR-MDR.PDF.

3 David Swanson, Twenty Dictators Currently Supported by the U.S., (Charlottesville, VA: David Swanson, 2020).

4 Jeffrey Ostler, Surviving Genocide: Native Nations and the United States from the American Revolution to Bleeding Kansas, (New Haven, CT: Yale University Press, 2020).

5 David Graeber and David Wengrow, The Dawn of Everything: A New History of Humanity, (New York, NY: Farrar, Straus, and Giroux, 2021).

6 David Swanson, "Treaties, Constitutions, and Laws Against War," *World Beyond War*, January 10, 2022, https://worldbeyondwar.org/constitutions/.

7 Matthew Waxman, "The Anniversary of the Monroe Doctrine," *Lawfare*, December 2, 2018, https://www.lawfareblog.com/anniversary-monroe-doctrine.

8 Chris Good, "President Obama's 'Red Line:' What He Actually Said About Syria and Chemical Weapons," *ABC News*, August 26, 2013, https://abcnews.go.com/blogs/politics/2013/08/president-obamas-red-line-what-he-actually-said-about-syria-and-chemical-weapons.

9 Admiral James "Sandy", Winnefeld Jr., "President Trump Draws His Red Line," *The Hill*, January 9, 2020, https://thehill.com/opinion/national-security/477469-president-trump-draws-a-red-line/.

10 "Doocy reveals President Biden's 'red line,'", *Fox News Business*, YouTube, March 14, 2022, https://www.youtube.com/watch?v=jyA7kJ_Z1rU.

11 Swanson, Twenty Dictators, op. cit.

12 "Press Release: At the OAS, Kerry Urges Region to Strengthen Democracies, Invest in Education, and Combat Climate Change," *OAS,* November 18, 2013, http://www.oas.org/en/media_center/press_release.asp?sCodigo=E-441/13.

13 "Kerry declares the end of the Monroe Doctrine era," *Al Jazeera America*, November 18, 2013, http://america.aljazeera.com/articles/2013/11/18/kerry-declares-theendofthemonroedoctrine.html

14 David Swanson, "U.S. Wars and Hostile Actions," *Let's Try Democracy: DavidSwanson.org*, January 8, 2023, https://davidswanson.org/warlist/.

15 Kerry J. Byrne, "On this day in history, December 2, 1823, President Monroe touts doctrine defending Western Hemisphere," *Fox News*, December 2, 2022, https://www.foxnews.com/lifestyle/this-day-history-dec-2-1823-president-monroe-touts-doctrine-western-hemisphere.

16 Robert O'Brien, "White House has to 'reinvoke' the Monroe Doctrine," *Fox News*, July 4, 2021, https://www.foxnews.com/video/6263671841001.

17 Robert Catenacci, "GOP Lawmakers blast Biden for turning to Venezuelan dictator for oil while curbing domestic production," *Fox Business*, November 29, 2022, https://www.foxbusiness.com/politics/gop-lawmakers-blast-biden-turning-venezuelan-dictator-oil-while-curbing-domestic-production.

18 A.L., "What is the Monroe Doctrine?" *The Economist,"* February 12, 2019, https://www.economist.com/the-economist-explains/2019/02/12/what-is-the-monroe-doctrine.

19 Adam Taylor, "What is the Monroe Doctrine? John Bolton's justification for Trump's push against Maduro," *The Washington* Post, March 4, 2019, https://www.washingtonpost.com/world/2019/03/04/what-is-monroe-doctrine-john-boltons-justification-trumps-push-against-maduro/.

20 Gautham Balaji, "Ukraine-Russia War: How Putin is using US's Monroe Doctrine against Nato," *India Today,* February 24, 2022, https://www.indiatoday.in/world/story/ukraine-russia-war-how-putin-is-using-us-s-monroe-doctrine-against-nato-1917135-2022-02-24.

21 Chen Qingqing and Xu Yelu, "Lavrov slams the US for global 'Monroe Doctrine' amid escalating tensions over Ukraine crisis," *Global Times*, September 26, 2022, https://www.globaltimes.cn/page/202209/1276075.shtml.

22 Tom Latek, "Changes approved for social studies curriculum," *The Herald Ledger,"* January 7, 2023, https://www.heraldledger.com/uncategorized/changes-approved-for-social-studies-curriculum/article_9d75cfa2-4e1d-57d5-a1c2-bb708d8997f1.html.

23 Kiron K. Skinner, Ph.D., "China Is Tightening Its Grip in America's Back Yard," *The Heritage Foundation,"* November 28, 2022, https://www.heritage.

org/asia/commentary/china-tightening-its-grip-americas-backyard.

24 James Carden, "Writing the Ukraine War History, As It Happens," *Responsible Statecraft*, November 30, 2022, https://responsiblestatecraft.org/2022/11/30/writing-the-ukraine-war-history-as-it-happens/.

25 Ellen Taylor, "A voice of sanity in the Ukraine war," *New Age: Opinion,* December 2, 2022, https://www.newagebd.net/article/188001/a-voice-of-sanity-in-ukraine-war.

26 Gretchen Murphy, Hemispheric Imaginings: The Monroe Doctrine and Narratives of U.S Empire (New Americanists), (Durham, NC: Duke University Press, 2005), vii.

27 Lucia Newman, "Trump revives Monroe Doctrine as warning to China and Russia," *Al Jazeera: News: Donald Trump,* June 19, 2019, https://www.aljazeera.com/news/2019/6/19/trump-revives-monroe-doctrine-as-warning-to-china-and-russia.

28 Adam Taylor, "What is the Monroe Doctrine?" *The Washington Post, March 4, 2019,* https://www.washingtonpost.com/world/2019/03/04/what-is-monroe-doctrine-john-boltons-justification-trumps-push-against-maduro/.

29 Ibid.

30 Vijay Prashad, "Africa Does Not Want to Be A Breeding Ground for the New Cold War: The Fourty-Forth Newsletter (2022)," *The Tricontinental*, November 3, 2022, https://thetricontinental.org/newsletterissue/africa-new-cold-war/.

31 David Swanson, host, "Talk World Radio: Allison Lira on U.S. Efforts Against Democracy in Honduras," *Talk World Radio: Let's Try Democracy: DavidSwanson.org,* (podcast), December 3, 2022, https://davidswanson.org/talk-world-radio-allison-lira-on-u-s-efforts-against-democracy-in-honduras/.

32 Jay Sexton, The Monroe Doctrine: Empire and Nation in 19th Century America, (New York, NY: Hill and Wang, 2012), 67.

33 Ibid., 121.

34 Patrick Greenfield and Phoebe Weston, "Cop15: Historic deal stuck to halt biodiversity loss by 2030", *The Guardian, December 19, 2022*, https://www.theguardian.com/environment/2022/dec/19/cop15-historic-deal-signed-to-halt-biodiversity-loss-by-2030-aoe.

35 H.W. Brands, "Presidential Doctrines: An Introduction," *JSTOR,* January 8, 2023, https://www.jstor.org/stable/27552741?read-now=1&oauth_data=eyJl

bWFpbCI6ImRhdmlkY25zd2Fuc29uQGdtYWlsLmNvbSIsImluc3RpdHV0aW9uSWRzIjpbXX0&seq=2#page_scan_tab_contents.

36 "United States presidential doctrines," Wikipedia, January 8, 2023, https://en.wikipedia.org/wiki/United_States_presidential_doctrines.

37 HNN Staff, "How Many Presidential Doctrines Have There Been?," *Columbia College of Arts and Sciences: History News Network*, January 8, 2023, https://historynewsnetwork.org/article/377.

38 Marc J. Selverstone, "Doctrines," *American Foreign Relations,* January 8, 2023, https://www.americanforeignrelations.com/A-D/Doctrines.html.

39 David Swanson, "Alternatives for the George Rogers Clark Monument at the University of Virginia," *Let's Try Democracy: DavidSwanson.org,* July 1, 2019, https://davidswanson.org/grc/.

40 Ostler, op. cit.

41 Murphy, op. cit. 42.

42 Ostler, op. cit.

43 Roxanne Dunbar-Ortiz, An indigenous People's History of the United States (Revisioning History), (Boston, MA: Beacon Press, 2015), 102.

44 David J. Toscano, Gene Sharp, et al, eds., Resistance, Politics, and the American Struggle for Independence, 1765-1775, (Lynne Rienner, 1986).

45 Howard Zinn, A People's History of the United States, (Harper Perennial Modern Classics, 2005).

46 David Swanson, host, "Talk Nation Radio: Robert Fantina on War and the Bravery of Deserters," *Talk World Radio: Let's Try Democracy: DavidSwanson.org,* (podcast), March 13, 2013, https://davidswanson.org/talk-nation-radio-robert-fantina-on-war-and-the-bravery-of-deserters-2/.

47 Ray Raphael, Founding Myths that Hide Our Patriotic Past, (New York, NY: The New Press, 2014).

48 David Swanson, host, "King George Was More Democratic Than American Revolutionaries," *Let's Try Democracy: DavidSwanson.org,* October 22, 2021, https://davidswanson.org/king-george-was-more-democratic-than-american-revolutionaries/.

49 Ibid.

50 Charles Dolgas, "Center for Government Contracting Wins Over $1 Million for Defense Finance Studies," *George Mason University: News,* June 22, 2021, https://www.gmu.edu/news/2021-12/center-government-contracting-

wins-over-1-million-defense-finance-studies.

51 Gary Hart, James Monroe: The American Presidents Series: The 5th President 1817-1825, (New York, NY: Times Books, 2005), 36.

52 Tim McGrath, James Monroe: A Life, (New York, NY: Dutton, 2020), 298.

53 Ibid., 300.

54 Ibid., 300-303.

55 Caitlin Gibson, "New research aims to connect Loudoun slaves to modern-day descendants," *The Washington Post,"* February 22, 2012, https://www.washingtonpost.com/local/new-research-aims-to-connect-loudoun-slaves-to-modern-day-descendants/2012/02/21/gIQApJcsTR_story.html.

56 Margaret Kimberly, Prejudential: Black America and the Presidents (Truth to Power), (Hanover, NH: Steerforth Press, 2020).

57 "Virginia Slaves Freed after 1782," *freeafricanamericans.com,* January 8, 2023, https://www.freeafricanamericans.com/virginiafreeafter1782.htm.

58 Stewart, David, "Burr on James Monroe," *David O. Stewart, Author and Speaker,* December 19. 2009, https://davidostewart.com/2009/12/19/burr_on_james_monroe/.

59 Hart, op. cit., 148.

60 Swanson, "U.S. Wars and Hostile Actions;" op. cit.

David Vine, The United States of War: A Global History of America's Endless Conflicts from Columbus to the Islamic State, (Volume 48) (California Series in Public Anthropology), (Oakland, CA: University of California Press, 2020);

William Appleman Williams, Empire as a Way of Life: Essays on the Causes and Character of America's Present Predicament Along With a Few Thoughts About an Alternative, (Oxford, England: Oxford University Press, 1980).

61 McGrath, op. cit., 475; Hart, op. cit. 79.

62 Hart, op. cit., 59.

63 Ibid., 100.

64 Sexton, op. cit., 61.

65 Graeber and Wingrow, op. cit.

66 Gregory Rehmke, "John Quincy Adams' July 4 Speech," *Economic Thinking,* July 4, 2007, updated July 4, 2017, https://economicthinking.org/john-quincy-adams-july-4-speec/.

67 Brian Concannon, Jr., and Mario Joseph, "Solidaridad?", *Counterpunch,* April 10, 2007, https://www.counterpunch.org/2007/04/10/solidaridad/.

68 McGrath, op. cit., 408.

69 Hart, op. cit., 114.

70 Ibid., 118.

71 Sexton, op. cit., 41.

72 Ibid., 11.

73 Hart, op. cit., 101.

74 Sexton, op. cit., 62.

75 Ibid., 63.

76 "Monroe Doctrine," *Wikipedia,* https://en.wikipedia.org/wiki/Monroe_Doctrine.

77 Sexton, op. cit., 68.

78 Ibid., 65.

79 Swanson, "US Wars and Hostile Actions," op. cit.;
Vine, The United States of War, op. cit.;
Williams, Empire as a Way of Life, op. cit.

80 Karl Berman, Under the Big Stick, (Compita Pub, 1986), 7.

81 Ibid.

82 Sexton, op. cit.

83 Polk, James K., "State of the Union Address (1845), December 2, 1845," *Teaching American History,* https://teachingamericanhistory.org/document/state-of-the-union-address-54/.

84 "Gen. Cass upon the Monroe Doctrine," January 20, 1853, *The New York Times,* https://timesmachine.nytimes.com/timesmachine/1853/01/20/75123992.html?pageNumber=4.

85 Murphy, op. cit., 62.

86 Sexton, op. cit., 118.

87 Berman, op. cit., 26.

88 Ibid., 44.

89 Ibid.

90 Sexton, op. cit., 156.

91 Eduardo Galeano, Open Veins of Latin America: Five Centuries of the Pillage of a Continent, (New York, NY: Monthly Review Press, 1997), 194.

92 Berman, op. cit., 11.

93 Ibid., 113.

94 Martí, José, "Inside the monster: writings on the United States and

American imperialism," *Internet Archive, 1975,* https://archive.org/details/insidemonsterwri00mart/page/339/mode/1up.

95 Cleveland, Grover, "December 17, 1895: Message Regarding Venezuelan-British Dispute," *UVA: Miller Center,* https://millercenter.org/the-presidency/presidential-speeches/december-17-1895-message-regarding-venezuelan-british-dispute.

96 David Swanson, "Among the World's Worst Events," *Let's Try Democracy: DavidSwanson.org,"* March 18, 2013, https://davidswanson.org/iraq.

97 Ibid.

98 Treaty Affairs Staff, Office of the Legal Advisor, U.S. Department of State, comp., "A List of Treaties and Other International Agreements of the United States in Force on January 1, 2020," *United States Department of State: state.gov,* https://www.state.gov/wp-content/uploads/2020/08/TIF-2020-Full-website-view.pdf.

99 "Treat Database: Overheid.NL," January 9, 2023, https://treatydatabase.overheid.nl/en/Treaty/Details/002330_b#United%20States%20of%20America.

100 Daniel Immerwahr, *Mother Jones*, "When Did the US Start Calling Itself 'America,' Anyway?" July 4, 2019, https://www.motherjones.com/politics/2019/07/when-did-the-united-states-start-calling-itself-america-anyway/

101 Sexton, op. cit., 228.

102 Charles F. Dole, "The Right and Wrong of the Monroe Doctrine," *The Atlantic: theAtlantic.com, April 1905,* https://www.theatlantic.com/magazine/archive/1905/04/the-right-and-wrong-of-the-monroe-doctrine/530856/.

103 "Theodore Roosevelt – Facts," *Peace: The Nobel Peace Prize 1906: Facts,* January 8, 2023, https://www.nobelprize.org/prizes/peace/1906/roosevelt/facts/.

104 Theodore Roosevelt, "Theodore Roosevelt: State of the Union 1904, 6 December 1904," *American History from Revolution to Reconstruction and Beyond,* January 8, 2023, https://www.let.rug.nl/usa/presidents/theodore-roosevelt/state-of-the-union-1904.php.

105 "Treaty Database," op. cit.

106 Galeano, op. cit., 107.

107 Jonathan Katz, Gangsters of Capitalism: Smedley Butler, the Marines, and the Making and Breaking of America's Empire (2021), (New York, NY: St. Martin's Press, 2022).

108 David Swanson, Leaving World War II Behind, (Charlottesville, VA: David

Swanson, 2020).

109 Gaddis Smith, "The Legacy of Monroe's Doctrine," *The New York Times, September 9, 1984,* https://www.nytimes.com/1984/09/09/magazine/the-legacy-of-monroes-doctrine.html.

110 J. Reuben Clark, Jr., (1973) "Appendix: The Clark Memorandum on the Monroe Doctrine," *BYU Studies Quarterly.* Vol. 13, Iss. 3, Article 14, https://scholarsarchive.byu.edu/cgi/viewcontent.cgi?article=1601&context=byusq.

111 Galeano, op. cit., 109.

112 David Swanson, "How Outlawing War Changed the World in 1928," *Let's Try Democracy: DavidSwanson.org,* September 12, 2017, https://davidswanson.org/how-outlawing-war-changed-the-world-in-1928/.

113 "The International Conference of American States: First Supplement: 1933-1940," (Washington, Carnegie Endowment for International Peace, 1940), https://www.oas.org/sap/peacefund/VirtualLibrary/EighthIntConfAmericanStates/Declarations/DeclarationofLima.pdf.

114 "The Monroe Doctrine (1939)," Patrick Reed on *YouTube,* January 8, 2023, https://www.youtube.com/watch?v=hfdMwusoUak.

115 Mary Jo McConahay, The Tango War: The Struggle for the Hearts, Minds and Riches of Latin America During World War II, (New York, NY: St. Martin's Press, 2018).

116 Berman, op. cit., 232.

117 William Boyd, "Hitler's amazing tap that turned America against the Nazis: A leading novelist's brilliant account of how British spies in the US staged a coup that helped drag Russia to war," *Daily Mail, June 28, 2014,* https://www.dailymail.co.uk/news/article-2673298/Hitlers-amazing-map-turned-America-against-Nazis-A-leading-novelists-brilliant-account-British-spies-US-staged-coup-helped-drag-Roosevelt-war.html.

118 "Hitler offers peace; Franco bids for Gibraltar; Konoye plays dictator," *Life* magazine, July 29, 1940, p. 20, *Google Books,* https://books.google.com/books?id=xz8EAAAAMBAJ&pg=PA20#v=onepage&q&f=false.

119 Harry S Truman, "March 12, 1947: Truman Doctrine," *UVA: Miller Center,* https://millercenter.org/the-presidency/presidential-speeches/march-12-1947-truman-doctrine.

120 Gaddis Smith, "Legacy," op. cit.

121 Dwight Eisenhower, "January 5, 1957: Eisenhower Doctrine," *UVA:*

Miller Center, https://millercenter.org/the-presidency/presidential-speeches/january-5-1957-eisenhower-doctrine.

122 85th Congress (1957-1958), "H.J.Res 117: Joint resolution to promote peace and stability in the Middle East," *Congress.gov,* https://www.congress.gov/bill/85th-congress/house-joint-resolution/117/text.

123 "The 2001 Authorization for the Use of Military Force: A Comprehensive Look at Where and How It Has Been Used," *Costs of War, Watson Institute, Brown University,* January 8, 2023, https://watson.brown.edu/costsofwar/papers/2021/2001AUMF.

124 "U.S. Stand Against Reds in Cuba Has Its Roots in Monroe Doctrine," *New York Times, April 19, 1961, Stanford.edu.,* https://web.stanford.edu/group/tomzgroup/pmwiki/uploads/0246-1961-04-19-PQ-c-sf.pdf.

125 "News Conference 24, August 29, 1961," *JFK Library,* January 8, 2023, https://www.jfklibrary.org/archives/other-resources/john-f-kennedy-press-conferences/news-conference-42.

126 John F. Kennedy, "Historic Speeches: Address During the Cuban Missile Crisis," October 22, 1962, *JFK Library,* https://www.jfklibrary.org/learn/about-jfk/historic-speeches/address-during-the-cuban-missile-crisis.

127 David Swanson, "Cuba Is Our Family," February 12, 2015, *Let's Try Democracy: DavidSwanson.org,* https://davidswanson.org/cuba-is-our-family/.

128 John F. Kennedy, "President Kennedy's Inaugural Address (1961)," *National Archives: Milestone Documents,* https://www.archives.gov/milestone-documents/president-john-f-kennedys-inaugural-address.

129 Gaddis Smith, "Legacy," op. cit.

130 William Blum, "Ecuador, 1960-1963: A Textbook of Dirty Tricks," *WilliamBlum.org,* https://williamblum.org/chapters/killing-hope/ecuador.

131 "Gen. Cass upon the Monroe Doctrine," op. cit.

132 Vincent Bevins, The Jakarta Method: Washington's Anti-Communist Crusade and the Mass Murder Program that Shaped Our World, (New York, NY, PublicAffairs, 2020), 91-111.

133 Mickey Z, There Is No Good War: The Myths of World War II, (Brooklyn: VoxPopNet, 2005), 110.

134 Lyndon B. Johnson, "Statement by the President Upon Ordering Troops into the Dominican Republic," April 28, 1965, *Presidency: UCSB.edu, https://www.presidency.ucsb.edu/documents/statement-the-president-upon-ordering-troops-*

into-the-dominican-republic;

Lyndon B. Johnson, "Radio and Television Report to the American People on the Situation in the Dominican Republic," May 2, 1965, *Presidency: UCSB.edu,* https://www.presidency.ucsb.edu/documents/radio-and-television-report-the-american-people-the-situation-the-dominican-republic.

135 David Swanson, War Is a Lie, (Chicago, IL: Just World Books, 2016), 66

136 Richard M. Nixon, "Address to the Nation on the War in Vietnam," November 3, 1969, *Internet Archives: Wayback Machine,* https://web.archive.org/web/20130124094303/http://www.nixonlibrary.gov/forkids/speechesforkids/silentmajority/silentmajority_transcript.pdf.

137 Naomi Klein, The Shock Doctrine: The Rise of Disaster Capitalism, (New York, NY: Metropolitan Books, 2007).

138 Bevins, op. cit.

139 Ibid., 266.

140 Select Committee to Study Government Operations with Respect to Intelligence Activities: United States Senate, "Covert Action in Chile: 1963-1973," (Washington, DC: U.S. Government Printing Office, 1975), https://www.aarclibrary.org/publib/church/reports/vol7/pdf/ChurchV7_13_Appendix.pdf.

141 "United States presidential doctrines," *Wikipedia, January 8, 2023,* https://en.wikipedia.org/wiki/United_States_presidential_doctrines.

142 Norman Solomon, War Made Easy: How Presidents and Pundits Keep Spinning Us to Death, (Hoboken, NJ: Wiley, 2006), 22-24.

143 Ibid., 12.

144 Robert Parry, "Bush's 'Death Squads,'" January 11, 2005, *Consortium News,* http://www.consortiumnews.com/2005/011105.html.

145 Berman, op. cit., 297.

146 James Reston, "Opinion: Washington; Reagan and Monroe," March 14, 1982, *The New York Times,* https://www.nytimes.com/1982/03/14/opinion/washington-reagan-and-monroe-by-james-reston.html.

147 "Congressional Record: Nomination of Robert M. Gates, of Virginia, to Be Director of Central Intelligence," November 5, 1991; *Intelligence Resource Program, Federation of American Scientists,* https://irp.fas.org/congress/1991_cr/s911105-gates2.htm.

148 Charles Krauthammer, "The Reagan Doctrine," *Time Magazine,* April 1, 1985, https://web.archive.org/web/20080209154146/http://www.time.com/

time/magazine/article/0,9171,964873,00.html.

149 "Solidarność (Solidarity) brings down the communist government of Poland, 1988-89," *Global Nonviolent Database,* January 8, 2023, https://nvdatabase.swarthmore.edu/index.php/content/solidarno-solidarity-brings-down-communist-government-poland-1988-89.

150 Swanson, "Treaties, Constitutions, and Laws Against War," op. cit.

151 Gaddis Smith, "Legacy," op. cit.

152 Ibid.

153 Ibid.

154 "The MacNeil/Lehrer Report; 6183; Interview with Caspar Weinberger," March 11, 1981, *American Archive of Public Broadcasting, https://americanarchive.org/catalog/cpb-aacip_507-zs2k64bt19*;

"Episode 20, Soldiers of Gold, Interview with Caspar Weinberger," August 1997, *Cold War Interviews, National Digital Security Archive,* https://nsarchive2.gwu.edu/coldwar/interviews/episode-20/weinberger3.html.

155 HNN Staff, op. cit.

156 "Contras," *Wikipedia,* January 8, 2023, https://en.wikipedia.org/wiki/Contras#cite_ref-51.

157 Gaddis Smith, The Last Years of the Monroe Doctrine, 1945-1993, (New York, NY: Hill and Wang, 1994), *Internet Archive,* January 8, 2023, https://archive.org/details/lastyearsofmonro0000smit/page/202/mode/2up.

158 Phyllis Schlafly, "Reaffirming the Monroe Doctrine – May 1987," *Phyllis Schlafly Eagles, The Phillis Schlafly Report,* January 8, 2023, https://www.phyllisschlafly.com/national-sovereignty/reaffirming-the-monroe-doctrine/.

159 "Human Rights Watch World Report 1989: Nicaragua," *Human Rights Watch, January 8, 2023, https://www.hrw.org/legacy/reports/1989/WR89/Nicaragu.htm*;

"Bush Vows to End Embargo if Chamorro Wins," *The Washington Post,* January 8, 2023, https://www.washingtonpost.com/archive/politics/1989/11/09/bush-vows-to-end-embargo-if-chamorro-wins/705463fe-b519-4cef-8e9e-95b2504081d6/.

160 "Most Notorious SOA Graduates," March 6, 2019, *SOA Watch,* https://soaw.org/notorious-soa-graduates.

161 Steven Lee Myers, "Be All That You Can Be: Your Future as an Extortionist," October 6, 1996, *The New York Times, https://www.nytimes.com/1996/10/06/*

weekinreview/be-all-that-you-can-be-your-future-as-an-extortionist.html;

"Prisoner Abuse: Patterns from the Past," National Security Archive Electronic Briefing Book #122, May 12, 2004, updated after February 25, 2014, *The National Security Archive, https://nsarchive2.gwu.edu/NSAEBB/NSAEBB122/*;

Beth Van Schaack, "The Torture Convention and Appendix M of the Army Field Manual on Interrogations," *Just Security,* https://www.justsecurity.org/18043/torture-convention-appendix-army-field-manual-interrogations/.

162 "US-trained ex-military intelligence officer sentenced to 22 years for murder of Berta Caceres," July 19, 2022, *School of the Americas Watch,* https://soaw.org/u-s-trained-ex-military-intelligence-officer-sentenced-to-22-years-for-murder-of-berta-caceres-2.

163 "Four WHINSEC graduates among those arrested for the assassination of President Moïse," July 22, 2021, *School of the Americas Watch,* https://soaw.org/whinsecgraduatesarrestedhaiti.

164 "SOA/WHINSEC graduate coup in Bolivia: US-backed regime massacres demonstrators," November 20, 2019, *School of the Americas Watch,* https://soaw.org/soa-whinsec-graduate-coup-in-bolivia-us-backed-regime-massacres-demonstrators.

165 HNN Staff, op. cit.

166 David Swanson, "Colin Powell's Own Staff Had Warned Him Against His War Lies," February 17, 2011, *Let's Try Democracy, DavidSwanson.org,* https://davidswanson.org/colin-powells-own-staff-had-warned-him-against-his-war-lies/.

167 David Swanson, "Humanitarian War vs. Humanity," February 23, 2011, *Let's Try Democracy, DavidSwanson.org,* https://davidswanson.org/humanitarian-war-vs-humanity/.

168 William Camacaro and Frederick Mills, "Decolonization and Multipolarity, and the Demise of the Monroe Doctrine," December 6, 2022, *Council on Hemispheric Affairs,* https://www.coha.org/decolonization-multipolarity-and-the-demise-of-the-monroe-doctrine/.

169 David Swanson, "Lies about Rwanda Mean More Wars if not Corrected," March 8, 2014, *Let's Try Democracy, DavidSwanson.org,* https://davidswanson.org/lies-about-rwanda-mean-more-wars-if-not-corrected/.

170 David Swanson, host, "Talk Nation Radio: Manuel Perez-Rocha: 20 Years of NAFTA is Enough," *Talk Nation Radio: Let's Try Democracy: DavidSwanson.*

org, (podcast), November 13, 2013, https://davidswanson.org/talk-nation-radio-manuel-perez-rocha-20-years-of-nafta-is-enough-3.

171 Tim Judson, "CAFTA Trade Lawsuit Highlights Threat to State Regulations from Bad Trade Agreements," August 26, 2010, *Institute for Agriculture & Trade Policy,"* https://www.iatp.org/news/cafta-trade-lawsuit-highlights-threat-to-state-regulations-from-bad-trade-agreements.

172 Swanson, "Allison Lira," op. cit.

173 Manual Perez-Rocha and Julia Paley, "What 'Free Trade' Has Done to Central America," November 21, 2015, *Foreign Policy in Focus,* https://fpif.org/free-trade-done-central-america;

Liz Grandia, et al, "Are corporations hog-tying conservation groups in CAFTA fight?" June 3, 2005, *Grist,* https://grist.org/article/grandia-cafta.

174 William Blum, "Haiti, 1986-1994: Who will rid me of this turbulent priest?" *WilliamBlum.org,* January 8, 2023, https://williamblum.org/chapters/killing-hope/haiti.

175 Ed Vulliamy, "Venezuela Coup Linked to Bush Team," April 21, 2002, *The Guardian: Observer World View,* https://www.theguardian.com/world/2002/apr/21/usa.venezuela.

176 Pablo Bachelet, "Bush Legacy: Farewell to the Monroe Doctrine?" March 1, 2008, *McClatchy-Tribune Information Services: McClatchy Newspaper: McClatchy Washington Bureau,* https://www.mcclatchydc.com/news/politics-government/article24477520.html.

177 Phil Stewart, "Ecuador wants military base in Miami," October 2, 2007, *Reuters,* https://www.reuters.com/article/ecuador-base-idUKADD25267520071022.

178 Florent Zemmouche, "In Conversation with Rafael Correa," July 18, 2022, *Latin American Information Agency (ALAI),* https://www.alai.info/en/in-conversation-with-rafael-correa/.

179 Alina Duarte, "The Nobodies Take Office in Colombia: An In-Depth Analysis," August 11, 2022, *Council on Hemispheric Affairs,* https://www.coha.org/the-nobodies-take-office-in-colombia-an-in-depth-analysis.

180 Dana Frank, "In Honduras, a Mess Made in the US," January 26, 2012, *The New York Times: Opinion, https://www.nytimes.com/2012/01/27/opinion/in-honduras-a-mess-helped-by-the-us.html*;

Karen Attiah, "Hilary Clinton's Dodgy Answers on Honduras Coup," April 19,

2016, *The Washington Post,* https://www.washingtonpost.com/blogs/post-partisan/wp/2016/04/19/hillary-clintons-dodgy-answers-on-honduras-coup/;

David Swanson, "Talk Nation Radio: Dana Frank on What the U.S. Is Doing to Honduras," January 22, 2019, *Let's Try Democracy, DavidSwanson.org,* (podcast), https://davidswanson.org/talk-nation-radio-dana-frank-on-what-the-u-s-is-doing-to-honduras.

181 Greg Grandin, "How Obama's Normalization of the Brazil Coup Prefigured Trumpism," November 22, 2016, *The Nation: Latin America,* https://www.thenation.com/article/archive/how-obamas-normalization-of-the-brazil-coup-prefigured-trumpism/.

182 "Trump Says He is Considering Military Action in Venezuela" (video), August 11, 2017, *Voice of America: Archive,* https://www.voanews.com/a/trump-military-action-venezuela/3982464.html.

183 Texas A&M University: U.S. Department of State YouTube Channels, "Secretary Pompeo Participates in Q&A Discussion at Texas A&M University," April 15, 2019, (video: 32:31) *YouTube,* https://www.youtube.com/watch?v=x6wbfjspVww&t=1700s;

Mark, Moore, "Venezuela could become a risk to US: CIA Director," April 13, 2017, *The New York Post,* https://nypost.com/2017/08/13/venezuela-could-become-a-risk-to-us-cia-director/.

184 "Economist Jeffrey Sachs: U.S. Sanctions Have Devastated Venezuela and Killed Over 40,000 Since 2017," May 1, 2019, (video), *Democracy Now,* https://www.democracynow.org/2019/5/1/economist_jeffrey_sachs_us_sanctions_have;

Max Blumenthal, "US regime change blueprint proposed Venezuelan electricity blackouts as 'water-shed event' for 'galvanizing public unrest,'" March 11, 2019, *The Gray Zone,* https://thegrayzone.com/2019/03/11/us-regime-change-blueprint-proposed-venezuelan-electricity-blackouts-as-watershed-event-for-galvanizing-public-unrest/.

185 Renzo, Pipoli, "Venezuela Oks Red Cross to transport humanitarian aid," March 29, 2019, *UPI: World News,* https://www.upi.com/Top_News/World-News/2019/03/29/Venezuela-OKs-Red-Cross-to-transport-humanitarian-aid/6391553881159/.

186 Jeb Sprague, "Washington's hybrid war on Venezuela – a very 21st century attempt at regime change," May 1, 2019, *Canary Workers' Co-op; Global;*

Opinion; US, https://www.thecanary.co/opinion/2019/05/01/washingtons-hybrid-war-on-venezuela-a-very-21st-century-attempt-at-regime-change;

"A War for Oil? Bolton Pushes Privatization of Venezuela's Oil as U.S. Ratchets Up Pressure on Maduro, January 30, 2019, (video), *Democracy Now,* https://www.democracynow.org/2019/1/30/a_war_for_oil_bolton_pushes.

187 Luis Fleischman, "Application of the Monroe Doctrine is a National and Regional Security Necessity," April 11, 2019, *Center for Security Policy,* https://centerforsecuritypolicy.org/application-of-the-monroe-doctrine-is-a-national-and-regional-security-necessity/.

188 Joshua Cho, "The Atlantic Illustrates Everything That's Wrong With Media's Coverage of Venezuela's Sanctions, May 6, 2019, *Fairness and Accuracy in Reporting (FAIR),* https://fair.org/home/the-atlantic-illustrates-everything-thats-wrong-with-media-coverage-of-venezuela-sanctions/;

Teddy Ostrow, "Zero Percent of Elite Commentators Oppose Regime Change in Venezuela," April 30, 2019, *Fairness and Accuracy in Reporting (FAIR),* https://fair.org/home/zero-percent-of-elite-commentators-oppose-regime-change-in-venezuela/;

Nicholas Casey, Christoph Koettl, and Deborah Acosta, "Footage Contradicts U.S. Claim That Nicolás Maduro Burned Aid Convoy," March 10, 2019, *The New York Times, https://www.nytimes.com/2019/03/10/world/americas/venezuela-aid-fire-video.html*;

Dave Lindorff, "Failed 'Coup' a Fake Corporate News Story Designed to Trick Venezuelan Soldiers – and US Public," May 7, 2019, *Fairness and Accuracy in Reporting (FAIR),* https://fair.org/home/failed-coup-a-fake-corporate-news-story-designed-to-trick-venezuelan-soldiers-and-us-public/;

Alan MacLeod, "Venezuela: It's Only a Coup if the US says so," May 1, 2019, *Fairness and Accuracy in Reporting (FAIR),* https://fair.org/home/venezuela-its-only-a-coup-if-the-us-government-says-so/.

189 French Hill, Obama Nearly Killed the Monroe Doctrine and Trump Should Revive it," April 6, 2017, *The Dallas Morning News,* https://www.dallasnews.com/opinion/commentary/2017/04/06/obama-nearly-killed-the-monroe-doctrine-and-trump-should-revive-it.

190 Brigette Gynther and Azadeh Shahshahani, "The White House's Plan to Stem Migration Protects Corporate Profit – Not People," August 2, 2022, *In These Times,* https://inthesetimes.com/article/kamala-harris-joe-biden-migration-

root-causes-central-america-corporate-profit.

191 Vijay Prashad and Jose Carlos Llerena, "The US egged on the coup in Peru," December 14, 2022, *The Morning Star for Peace and Socialism, https://www*.morningstaronline.co.uk/article/f/us-egged-coup-peru.

192 Bret Wilkins (Common Dreams), "Sanders, Kain Hail US Senate Passage of Brazil Election Resolution," September 28, 2022, *Bernie Sanders: US Senator for Vermont, https://www*.sanders.senate.gov/in-the-news/sanders-kaine-hail-us-senates-passage-of-brazil-election-resolution.

Senator Tim Kaine, "*CAN22736 6XH*. S.L.C.. 117TH CONGRESS. 2D SESSION. S. RES. ll. Urging the Government of Brazil to ensure that the October 2022 elections," October 2, 2022, https://www.kaine.senate.gov/imo/media/doc/brazil_resolution.pdf.

193 "Mapping Militarism," *World Beyond War,* https://worldbeyondwar.org/militarism-mapped/.

194 Meredith Bennett-Smith, "Womp! This Country Was Named The Greatest Threat To World Peace," January 23, 2014, *HuffPost*, https://www.huffingtonpost.com/2014/01/02/greatest-threat-world-peace-country_n_4531824.html (January 23, 2014).

195 Dorothy Manevich and Hanyu Chwe, "Globally, more people see U.S. power and influence as a major threat," August 1, 2017, *Pew Research Center,* http://www.pewresearch.org/fact-tank/2017/08/01/u-s-power-and-influence-increasingly-seen-as-threat-in-other-countries.

196 Thank you to David Vine, William Appleman Williams, and others who have drawn up such lists, which I have compiled at https://davidswanson.org/warlist.

197 Daniel Immerwahr, How to Hide an Empire: A History of the Greater United States, (London, England: Picador, 2020).

198 James Bradley, Imperial Cruise, (Boston, MA: Back Bay Books, 2010).

199 Neil Smith, The Endgame of Globalization, (Abingdon, Oxfordshire, England: Taylor and Francis/Routledge, 2005), Kindle Edition, 73.

200 Ibid., 69.

201 Stephen Wertheim, Tomorrow, The World: The Birth of U.S. Global Supremacy, (Cambridge, MA: Harvard University Press/Belknap Press, 2022).

202 Rachel Maddow Presents, "Transcript: The Brooklyn Boys," MSNBC, Oct. 10, 2022, https://www.msnbc.com/msnbc-podcast/rachel-maddow-presents-

ultra/transcript-brooklyn-boys-n1299419

203 Rachel Maddow Presents, "Ultra," MSNBC, 2022, https://www.msnbc.com/rachel-maddow-presents-ultra

204 Teddy Ostrow, "WSJ Sells Lithium Neocolonialism as Climate Necessity," August 23, 2022, *Fairness and Accuracy in Reporting (FAIR),* https://fair.org/home/wsj-sells-lithium-neocolonialism-as-climate-necessity.

205 Ben Norton, Multipolarista, "Biden Official: U.S. Would Have Plotted a Coup 40 Years Ago," August 18, 2022, *Popular Resistance: Daily Movement News and Resources,* https://popularresistance.org/top-biden-official-us-would-overthrow-colombias-new-left-wing-president-40-years-ago.

Fabián Ramírez, ed., Juan González: "Hace 40 años, EE. UU. hubiera hecho todo lo possible para prevenir elección de Petro," *Noticias.Caracol,* https://noticias.caracoltv.com/economia/juan-gonzalez-hace-40-anos-ee-uu-hubiera-hecho-todo-lo-posible-para-prevenir-eleccion-de-petro-rg10.

206 Andrés Manuel López Obrador, "Discurso del president Andrés Manuel López Obrador en el 238 Aniversario del Natalicio de Simón Bolívar, desde el Castillo de Chapultepec," July 24, 2021, *AMLO,* https://lopezobrador.org.mx/2021/07/24/discurso-del-presidente-andres-manuel-lopez-obrador-en-el-238-aniversario-del-natalicio-de-simon-bolivar-desde-el-castillo-de-chapultepec.

207 David Swanson, Best National Government in North America: Mexico," August 8, 2018, *Let's Try Democracy: DavidSwanson.org,* https://davidswanson.org/best-national-government-in-north-america-mexico.

208 David Swanson, "President of Mexico Declines Trump's Offer of a War," November 5, 2019, *Let's Try Democracy: DavidSwanson.org,* https://davidswanson.org/president-of-mexico-declines-trumps-offer-of-a-war.

209 *William* Camacaro and Frederick Mills, "Decolonization, Multipolarity,, and the Demise of the Monroe Doctrine," December 6, 2022, *Council on Hemispheric Affairs,* https://www.coha.org/decolonization-multipolarity-and-the-demise-of-the-monroe-doctrine.

Nino Pagliccia, "The Death of the 'Lima Group' and Re-Birth of the Latin American Anti-Imperialist Left," August 17, 2021, *Counterpunch,* https://www.counterpunch.org/2021/08/17/the-death-of-the-lima-group-and-re-birth-of-the-latin-american-anti-imperialist-left.

210 "Declaración de Santa Marta: 'La Región, Unida por el Cambio –

Noviembre 2022,'" November 11, 2022, *Grupo de Puebla,* https://www.grupodepuebla.org/en/declaraciondesantamarta.

211 Camarco and Mills, op. cit.

212 "Declaración del II Encuentro de Abyea Yala Soberana," November 30, 2022, *Abya Yala Soberana,* https://abyayalasoberana.org/movilizacion/declaracion-del-ii-encuentro-de-abya-yala-soberana/.

213 Claudio Garcia-Rojas, "Incarcerating Nations: On the Dangers of Exporting US Prison Systems," August 15, 2016, *Truthout,* https://truthout.org/articles/incarceration-nations-on-the-dangers-of-exporting-us-prison-systems.

Baz Dreisinger, "Prison: America's Most Vile Export?" September 30, 2015, *The Atlantic,* https://www.theatlantic.com/international/archive/2015/09/us-world-prisons-supermax-incarceration/408067.

214 David Swanson, "Re-Joining the World," January 15, 2021, *Let's Try Democracy: DavidSwanson.org,* https://davidswanson.org/re-joining-the-world/.

215 Max Rennebohm, researcher, "Chileans overthrow dictator Carlos Ibañez del Campo, 1931," September 21, 2009, *Global Nonviolent Action Database,* https://nvdatabase.swarthmore.edu/index.php/content/chileans-overthrow-dictator-carlos-iba-ez-del-campo-1931.

216 Max Rennebohm, ed., "Cuban's general strike to overthrow president, 1933," June 15, 2011, *Global Nonviolent Action Database,* https://nvdatabase.swarthmore.edu/index.php/content/cubans-general-strike-overthrow-president-1933.

Max Rennebohm, ed., "Cuban's general strike to overthrow president, 1935," June 5, 2011, *Global Nonviolent Action Database,* https://nvdatabase.swarthmore.edu/index.php/content/cubans-general-strike-overthrow-president-1935.

217 The overthrow of the military regime in El Salvador in 1944 is recounted in *A Force More Powerful.*

Max Rennebohm, ed., "El Salvadorans bring down a dictator, 1944," October 9, 2011, *Global Nonviolent Action Database,* *https://nvdatabase.swarthmore.edu/index.php/content/el-salvadorans-bring-down-dictator-1944.*

Max Rennebohm, ed., "Guatemalans overthrow a dictator, 1944," May 18, 2011, *Global Nonviolent Action Database,* *https://nvdatabase.swarthmore.edu/index.php/content/guatemalans-overthrow-dictator-1944.*

Kate McClellan, researcher, "Ecuadorians overthrow dictator (Glorious May Revolution), 1944," June 11, 2011, *Global Nonviolent Action Database,* https://nvdatabase.swarthmore.edu/index.php/content/ecuadorians-overthrow-dictator-glorious-may-revolution-1944.

218 Max Rennebohm, researcher, "Haitians overthrow a dictator, 1946," November 29, 2009, *Global Nonviolent Action Database,* https://nvdatabase.swarthmore.edu/index.php/content/haitians-overthrow-dictator-1946

219 Max Rennebohm, researcher, "Colombians overthrow dictator, 1957," June 12, 2009, *Global Nonviolent Action Database,* https://nvdatabase.swarthmore.edu/index.php/content/colombians-overthrow-dictator-1957.

220 See account in Part 1 of "Civil Resistance Against Coups" by Stephen Zunes.

Stephen Zunes, "Civil Resistance Against Coups: A Comparative and Historical Perspective," 2017, *International Center on Nonviolent Conflict: ICNC Monograph Series,* https://www.nonviolent-conflict.org/wp-content/uploads/2017/11/Stephen-Zunes-Monograph_Final-for-online_HGS_Apr_9.pdf.

221 Max Rennebohm, ed., "Mothers of the Plaza de Mayo campaign for democracy and the return of their 'disappeared' family members, 1977-1983," September 10, 2011, *Global Nonviolent Action Database,* https://nvdatabase.swarthmore.edu/index.php/content/mothers-plaza-de-mayo-campaign-democracy-and-return-their-disappeared-family-members-1977-19.

222 Max Rennebohm, ed., "Uruguayans general strike against the military government, 1984," April 19, 2011, *Global Nonviolent Action Database,* https://nvdatabase.swarthmore.edu/index.php/content/uruguayans-general-strike-against-military-government-1984.

223 See account in Part 1 of "Civil Resistance Against Coups" by Stephen Zunes.

Zunes, op. cit.

224 Shandra Bernath-Plaistad and Max Rennebohm, researchers, "Chileans overthrow Pinochet regime, 1983-1988," October 31, 2008 and July 9, 2011, *Global Nonviolent Action Database,* https://nvdatabase.swarthmore.edu/index.php/content/chileans-overthrow-pinochet-regime-1983-1988.

225 Jamie Irwin, "Brazilians drive out corrupt president – 1992," February 15, 2015, *Global Nonviolent Action Database,* https://nvdatabase.swarthmore.edu/index.php/content/brazilians-drive-out-corrupt-president-1992.

226 Max Rennebohm, ed., "Peruvians campaign to overthrow dictator Alberto Fujimori (The March of the Four Directions), 2000," February 6, 2011, *Global Nonviolent Action Database,* https://nvdatabase.swarthmore.edu/index.php/content/peruvians-campaign-overthrow-dictator-alberto-fujimori-march-four-directions-2000.

227 Nick Palazzolo "Ecuadorians oust President Gutiérrez (Rebellion of the Forajidos), 2005," February 17, 2013, *Global Nonviolent Action Database,* https://nvdatabase.swarthmore.edu/index.php/content/ecuadorians-oust-president-guti-rrez-rebellion-forajidos-2005.

228 *Under Rich Earth,* (Human Rights Watch, 2008) 0.92., https://ff.hrw.org/film/under-rich-earth.

229 Irina Bukharin, researcher, "Guatemalans force corrupt president and VP to resign, 2015," October 25, 2015, *Global Nonviolent Action Database,* https://nvdatabase.swarthmore.edu/index.php/content/guatemalans-force-corrupt-president-and-vp-resign-2015.

230 "Communidad de Paz de San José de Apartadó," February 2015, *Publicado por Peace Direct; Peace Insight, https://www.peaceinsight.org/es/organisations/peace-village-of-san-jose-de-apartado/?location=colombia&theme.*

"Peace Community of San José de Apartadó," *For Peace Presence,* January 8, 2023, https://peacepresence.org/what-we-do/peace-community/.

"Peace Community of San José de Apartadó," *Tamera,* January 8, 2023, https://www.tamera.org/peace-community-colombia/.

231 "Las Abejas," *Wikipedia,* January 8, 2023, https://en.wikipedia.org/wiki/Las_Abejas.

"La Sociedad Civil las Abejas de Acteal Recibirán Premil a la Defensa Ambiental en Chiapas Mariano Abarca 2021, 27 de Noviembre 2021," January 8, 2023, *Otros Mundos AC Chiapas,* https://otrosmundoschiapas.org/las-abejas-de-acteal-recibiran-el-premio-a-la-defensa-ambiental-en-chiapas-mariano-abarca-2021.

Andalusia Knoll, "Acteal, Mexico: Building Autonomy in the Shadow of Repression," *Las Abejas de Acteal,* January 8, 2023, http://acteal.blogspot.com/p/english.html.

232 Rachel Small, "Why I'm Going to the Frontlines of the Wet'suwet'en Resistance," October 27, 2021, *World BEYOND War,* https://worldbeyondwar.org/why-im-going-to-the-frontlines-of-the-wetsuweten-resistance/.

233 Brad Evans, (2009), "Revolution Without Violence," *Peace Review,* 21:1,

85-94, *Routledge: Taylor & Francis Group,* https://www.tandfonline.com/doi/pdf/10.1080/10402650802690110.

David Swanson, "Film: Costa Rica Abolished Its Military, Never Regretted It," June 4, 2015, *Let's Try Democracy: DavidSwanson.org,* https://davidswanson.org/film-costa-rica-abolished-its-military-never-regretted-it/.

234 Francesca Lessa, "Operation Condor: Why victims of the oppression that swept 1970's South America are still fighting for justice," *https://theconversation.com/operation-condor-why-victims-of-the-oppression-that-swept-1970s-south-america-are-still-fighting-for-justice-186789.*

235 David Swanson, "Where there were massacres there are now power plants," September 16, 2015., *Let's Try Democracy: DavidSwanson.org,* https://davidswanson.org/where-there-were-massacres-there-are-now-power-plants/.

Jo-Marie Burt and Paulo Estrada/ELFARO, "Trial for 'Death Squad Dossier' Ties Guatemalan Wartime Atrocities to Current Criminal Networks," April 25, 2022, *Portside,* https://portside.org/2022-04-25/trial-death-squad-dossier-ties-guatemalan-wartime-atrocities-current-criminal-networks.

236 Juan Pablo Lazo Ureta, "For an Era of Peace: Ongoing History of an Initiative to Abolish War as a Constitutional Precept in Chile," December 27, 2021, *World Beyond War,* https://worldbeyondwar.org/for-an-era-of-peace-ongoing-history-of-an-initiative-to-abolish-war-as-a-constitutional-precept-in-chile/.

237 "The Quest to Defuse Guyana's Carbon Bomb": Meet the Environmental Lawyer Taking on ExxonMobil" (transcript), December 23, 2022, *Democracy Now,* https://www.democracynow.org/2022/12/23/guyanas_carbon_bomb_exxonmobil#transcript.

238 "Evo Morales: NATO Is a Threat to the World; Must Be Dissolved," (video) March 10, 2022, *teleSUR,* https://www.telesurenglish.net/news/Evo-Morales-NATO-Is-a-Threat-to-the-World-Must-Be-Dissolved-20220310-0004.html.

239 Karl, Walling, review of Joseph M. Syracusa and Aiden Warren, Presidential Doctrines: U.S. National Security from George Washington to Barack Obama, (New York: Rowman & Littlefield, 2016), *University of Chicago Press Journals, American Political Thought: vol.7, no. 3, Summer 2018,* https://www.journals.uchicago.edu/doi/10.1086/698491.

240 David Swanson, "A Forgotten RNC," August 25, 2012, *Let's Try Democracy: DavidSwanson.org,* https://davidswanson.org/a-forgotten-rnc/.

241 David Swanson, "The Best Speech Yet from Any U.S. President," September 18, 2017, *Let's Try Democracy: DavidSwanson.org,* https://davidswanson.org/the-best-speech-yet-from-any-u-s-president/.

242 Peter Kornbluh, ed., "The Cuban Missile Crisis @ 60: John F. Kennedy Sacrificed His Most Consequential Crisis Advisor," October 17, 2022, *National Security Archive,* https://nsarchive.gwu.edu/briefing-book/cuba-cuban-missile-crisis/2022-10-17/cuban-missile-crisis-60-how-john-f-kennedy.

CPSIA information can be obtained
at www.ICGtesting.com
Printed in the USA
BVHW081057120323
660180BV00010B/631

9 798986 981109